Take Control

Controls the SOURCE. Controls the SYMPTOM. Controls the SEASON.

ALOCRIL® ophthalmic solution gives patients continuous symptom control beyond relief—
on the greens, off the greens, all season long.

Frequently reported adverse events included headache, irritation, nasal congestion, ocular burning, stinging, and unpleasant taste in ten to forty percent of patients. Other events occurring between one and ten percent included asthma, conjunctivitis, eye redness, photophobia, and rhinitis. Some of these events were similar to those produced by the underlying ocular disease being studied.

For the treatment of ocular itch due to allergic conjunctivitis.

Please see accompanying full prescribing information.

Alocril.
(nedocromil sodium ophthalmic solution) 2%

TAKE CONTROL

ALOCRIL® (nedocromil sodium ophthalmic solution) 2%
Sterile

DESCRIPTION
ALOCRIL® (nedocromil sodium ophthalmic solution) 2% is a clear, yellow, sterile solution for topical ophthalmic use.

Nedocromil sodium is represented by the following structural formula:

$C_{19}H_{15}NNa_2O_7$ Mol. Wt. 415.30   CAS: 69049-74-7

Chemical Name: 4H-Pyrano[3,2-g] quinoline-2, 8-dicarboxylic acid, 9-ethyl-6, 9-dihydro-4, 6-dioxo-10-propyl-, disodium salt.

Each mL Contains: Active: Nedocromil sodium 20 mg (2%); **Preservative:** Benzalkonium chloride 0.01%; **Inactives:** Sodium chloride 0.5%, edetate disodium 0.05% and purified water. It has a pH of 4.0 to 5.5.

CLINICAL PHARMACOLOGY
Nedocromil sodium is a mast cell stabilizer. Nedocromil sodium inhibits the release of mediators from cells involved in hypersensitivity reactions. Decreased chemotaxis and decreased activation of eosinophils have also been demonstrated.

In vitro studies with adult human bronchoalveolar cells showed that nedocromil sodium inhibits histamine release from a population of mast cells having been defined as belonging to the mucosal sub type and beta-glucuronidase release from macrophages.

Pharmacokinetics and Bioavailability
Nedocromil sodium exhibits low systemic absorption. When administered as a 2% ophthalmic solution in adult human volunteers, less than 4% of the total dose was systemically absorbed following multiple dosing. Absorption is mainly through the nasolacrimal duct rather than through the conjunctiva. It is not metabolized and is eliminated primarily unchanged in urine (70%) and feces (30%).

INDICATIONS AND USAGE
ALOCRIL® is indicated for the treatment of itching associated with allergic conjunctivitis.

CONTRAINDICATIONS
ALOCRIL® is contraindicated in those patients who have shown hypersensitivity to nedocromil sodium or to any of the other ingredients.

PRECAUTIONS
Information for Patients
Patients should be advised to follow the patient instructions listed on the Information for Patients sheet.

Users of contact lenses should refrain from wearing lenses while exhibiting the signs and symptoms of allergic conjunctivitis.

Carcinogenesis, Mutagenesis, and Impairment of Fertility
A two-year inhalation carcinogenicity study of nedocromil sodium at a dose of 24 mg/kg/day (approximately 400 times the maximum recommended human daily ocular dose on a mg/kg basis) in Wistar rats showed no carcinogenic potential.

Nedocromil sodium showed no mutagenic potential in the Ames Salmonella/microsome plate assay, mitotic gene conversion in *Saccharomyces cerevisiae*, mouse lymphoma forward mutation and mouse micronucleus assays.

Reproduction and fertility studies in mice and rats showed no effects on male and female fertility at a subcutaneous dose of 100 mg/kg/day (more than 1600 times the maximum recommended human daily ocular dose).

Pregnancy: Teratogenic Effects: Pregnancy Category B
Reproduction studies performed in mice, rats and rabbits using a subcutaneous dose of 100 mg/kg/day (more than 1600 times the maximum human daily ocular dose on a mg/kg basis) revealed no evidence of teratogenicity or harm to the fetus due to nedocromil sodium. There are, however, no adequate and well-controlled studies in pregnant women. Because animal reproduction studies are not always predictive of human response, ALOCRIL® should be used during pregnancy only if clearly needed.

Nursing Mothers
After intravenous administration to lactating rats, nedocromil was excreted in milk. It is not known whether this drug is excreted in human milk. Because many drugs are excreted in human milk, caution should be exercised when ALOCRIL® is administered to a nursing woman.

Pediatric Use
Safety and effectiveness in children below the age of 3 years have not been established.

Geriatric Use
No overall differences in safety or effectiveness have been observed between elderly and younger patients.

ADVERSE REACTIONS
The most frequently reported adverse experience was headache (~40%).

Ocular burning, irritation and stinging, unpleasant taste, and nasal congestion have been reported to occur in 10 - 30% of patients. Other events occurring between 1 - 10% included asthma, conjunctivitis, eye redness, photophobia, and rhinitis.

Some of these events were similar to the underlying ocular disease being studied.

DOSAGE AND ADMINISTRATION
The recommended dosage is one or two drops in each eye twice a day. ALOCRIL® should be used at regular intervals.

Treatment should be continued throughout the period of exposure (i.e., until the pollen season is over or until exposure to the offending allergen is terminated), even when symptoms are absent.

HOW SUPPLIED
ALOCRIL® (nedocromil sodium ophthalmic solution) 2% is supplied as 5 mL of solution in a natural, low-density polyethylene round eye drop bottle with a controlled dropper tip, and a natural polypropylene cap.

5 mL   NDC 0023-8842-05

Storage
Store between 2° - 25°C (36° - 77°F). Keep tightly closed and out of the reach of children.

Rx Only

Manufactured by
Laboratoires FISONS SA
Le Trait, France

Distributed by
Allergan
Irvine, CA 92612, USA
©2000 Allergan, Inc.

® Marks owned by Allergan, Inc.
U.S. Pat.: 4,760,072; 4,474,787; and 5,443,833.

 ALLERGAN

71338US11H
8729X

AMERICAN GOLF COURSES

America's Most Challenging Public Golf Courses

JIM MORIARTY

Foreword by Robert Trent Jones, Sr.

TODTRI

This book was designed and published by
TODTRI Book Publishers
254 West 31st Street, New York, NY 10001-2813
Fax: (212) 695-6984 E-mail: info@todtri.com

Visit us on the web!
www.todtri.com

Printed and Bound in Singapore

Library of Congress Catalog Card Number 91-072521

ISBN 1-57717-204-3

Author: Jim Moriarty
Producer: Robert M. Tod
Designer and Art Director: Mark Weinberg
Editor: Mary Forsell
Typeset and Page Makeup: Strong Silent Type/NYC

TABLE OF CONTENTS

1. **Arrowhead,** *Colorado*
2. **Banff Springs,** *Alberta, Canada*
3. **Barton Creek,** *Texas*
4. **Bethpage Black,** *New York*
5. **Blackwolf Run,** *Wisconsin*
6. **The Boulders,** *Arizona*
7. **Boyne Highlands,** *Michigan*
8. **Breckenridge,** *Colorado*
9. **The Broadmoor,** *Colorado*
10. **Cantigny,** *Illinois*
11. **Carambola,** *Virgin Islands*
12. **Casa de Campo,** *Dominican Republic*
13. **Cog Hill,** *Illinois*
14. **Concord,** *New York*
15. **Desert Dunes,** *California*
16. **Desert Inn,** *Nevada*
17. **Doral,** *Florida*
18. **Edgewood Tahoe,** *Nevada*
19. **Glen Abbey,** *Ontario, Canada*
20. **Grand Cypress,** *Florida*
21. **Grand Traverse,** *Michigan*
22. **The Greenbrier,** *West Virginia*
23. **Harbour Town,** *South Carolina*
24. **Heather Glen,** *South Carolina*
25. **Heritage,** *South Carolina*
26. **The Homestead,** *Virginia*
27. **Hominy Hill,** *New Jersey*
28. **Horseshoe Bay,** *Texas*
29. **Innisbrook,** *Florida*
30. **Jackson Hole,** *Wyoming*
31. **Jasper Park,** *Alberta, Canada*
32. **Kananaskis,** *Alberta, Canada*
33. **Kemper Lakes,** *Illinois*
34. **Kiawah,** *South Carolina*
35. **Kingsmill,** *Virginia*
36. **La Costa,** *California*
37. **Las Hadas,** *Mexico*
38. **Mauna Kea,** *Hawaii*
39. **Mauna Lani,** *Hawaii*
40. **Pasatiempo Golf Club,** *California*
41. **Pebble Beach Golf Links,** *California*
42. **PGA West,** *California*
43. **Pinehurst No. 2,** *North Carolina*
44. **Pinehurst No. 7,** *North Carolina*
45. **The Pit Golf Links,** *North Carolina*
46. **Sea Island,** *Georgia*
47. **Semiahmoo,** *Washington*
48. **Spanish Bay,** *California*
49. **Spyglass,** *California*
50. **Tanglewood Park,** *North Carolina*
51. **Teton Pines,** *Wyoming*
52. **Tidewater,** *South Carolina*
53. **Tokatee,** *Oregon*
54. **Torrey Pines,** *California*
55. **Tournament Players Club,** *Florida*
56. **Tournament Players Club,** *Arizona*
57. **Troon North,** *Arizona*
58. **Tryall,** *West Indies*
59. **Ventana Canyon,** *Arizona*
60. **Wild Dunes,** *South Carolina*

INTRODUCTION

It's one of the pities of this frustrating and magnificent game that so many of the great golf courses are inaccessible to the vast public who support it. Fortunately for us all, this is not always the case. What follows is a compendium of those places that you and I can play, from Pebble Beach to Doral, Banff to Casa de Campo.

This is by no means the definitive list, the irrefutable sixty. Culling the list to that number proved to be a daunting task. Sometimes it seemed as if there are enough excellent resort and public courses to make up two or three books. If your particular favorite is missing, I apologize. I'm sure it deserves to be here, too.

I have tried to include a variety of courses. Some of them are very expensive and can only be played if you're staying on the grounds. But I felt it was also important to include courses where you can walk up to the pro shop counter, pay your money, and tee it up.

We're hoping thats exactly what you will do.

J.M.

FOREWORD

As a golfer who took his first tentative strokes on a public course and as one who developed it to a point that par was not a mystery, I always have had a warm spot in my heart for pay-as-you-play golf and the courses that make it possible.

My high regard for daily-fee layouts goes even further. How could it be otherwise when the first golf course to bear my design signature was the Midvale Golf Club, a public course in Rochester, New York, a town in which I grew up.

It was an accomplishment that sent me on my way, and in the sixty years that have intervened and the more than 450 golf courses for which I have been responsible, I never have lost sight of the fact that public links golf is the true grassroots of the game.

In contrast to my long-ago exposure to public links golf back during the first golf boom in the '20s when only a meager ten percent of the courses were on a daily-fee basis, today the more than 13,000 layouts in the United States are predominately facilities available to anybody with a set of clubs or a desire to try what has been termed the most humbling of games.

And what difference there is today in the quality of the public courses, in sharp contrast to what they were during the day Bobby Jones was making the headlines as the game's greatest player. Many of todays public courses are the equal of the best of the private layouts in challenge and conditioning a far cry from their ancient predecessors, which in the main seldom were blessed with any water except that which nature provided, were rife with more weeds than grass, and of such a design as to warrant the derisive description of public golf as cow pasture pool.

Despite the fact there are nearly 8,000 public courses of every description municipal, county, and state, and hundreds of privately owned there still are not enough, so popular has this game become in the last decade. Included in this book is a great collection which, conceivably, could serve as nucleus of anybodys one hundred best, which such PGA Tour stops as Pebble Beach; Spyglass Hill; Torrey Pines; Harbour Town; the Tournament Players Club; Pinehurst No. 2; Kingsmill; and the new Ocean Course on Kiawah Island where the 1991 Ryder Cup Match was played along with the PGA Wests Stadium course, annual site of the Skins Game; and Tanglewood Park, where the Senior PGA Tour holds the Vantage Cup, the richest even on this schedule.

Knowing of the high standards and the playability requirements employed by the author in assembling his list, I am sure any golfer who uses it as a guide will not be disappointed.

Robert Trent Jones.

Robert Trent Jones

Arrowhead
Colorado

Stunning mountain vistas. Stark desert terrain. The rumble of the ocean at a seaside links. Many of the courses appearing in this book are set in landscapes of breathtaking beauty, but none is more unusual or striking than Arrowhead Golf Club in Littleton, Colorado.

In the golden early morning light the jagged red rock pinnacles seem to jut from the earth like giant rows of red piranha teeth. This captivating geological sandstone formation was created some 270 million years ago at the foot of the Rocky Mountains. Robert Trent Jones Jr. has exploited it with loving care as the setting of this 6,682-yard, par 70 golf course.

Unlike some courses where there are, for example, a combination of "marsh" holes and "ocean" holes, Arrowhead never gives you that feeling of separation. Certainly, there are occasions when you're playing much closer to the sheer rock faces than others. Yet the overall feeling is more like entering a cathedral than going from, say, boxcar to boxcar. From the very first shot, it's as if you're surrounded by a mystical piece of ground. You'll spend as much time taking in the landscape as you will thinking about your game.

Remember, you've got some altitude here so the yardages are not quite what they seem. You're also not way up in the Rockies, however. Club selection will be a bit tricky. I'd suggest coming off one full club to start and adjust up or down from there.

The 1st is among the toughest holes you'll play all day. It's 453 yards with nasty little clumps of trees right and left, a bunker on the right side of the fairway, and a green protected by water and bunkers (it's a double green, shared with the incoming 17th). The sandstones tower on your left.

The truth is, the front nine has a murderous selection of four pars. Along with the 1st, the 436-yard 4th is a devil with a row of fairway bunkers, trees, water,

Arrowhead takes its name from the towering red rocks behind the 11th green.

a ravine, and an elevated green up against the rocks. At 454 yards, the 6th is long and can be gruesome. The 8th is 412 yards of threading the needle between trees and bunkers and rocks.

On the back nine the view from the 10th tee, overlooking the rows and rows of red pinnacles toward Roxborough State Park, is one of the prettiest vistas in golf. The 11th green is set at the base of the rock formation from which the golf course takes its name.

The three-hole finish at Arrowhead gives you two par fives, the 578-yard 16th and the 543-yard 18th, sandwiched around the one-shot, 204-yard 17th. The 18th is a dangerous closing hole with water along the left for the final 250 or so yards, but it can be reached with two precise shots. It's a good chance to finish with a birdie and cap off a beautiful round.

The third green is rimmed by a red rock formation. If you miss to the right the ball winds up on the 4th tee.

Banff Springs
Alberta, Canada

No sport has more shrines than golf. And there is no more inspiring shrine than Banff Springs. Pressed snugly into the Canadian Rockies, you may see elk or moose wading through the water hazards or climbers rappelling on a sheer mountain face that seems to rise directly out of the semirough.

The original golf course was built in 1927 by Canadian architect Stanley Thompson, the mentor of Robert Trent Jones. An additional nine holes by Bill Robinson were added recently, and though highly compatible, you'll want to play the Thompson course. Banff Springs is in the Banff National Park, and the season runs from about the first of May until around the middle of October, plus or minus. In the long summer's twilight it's possible to play until after 10 p.m. When the course shuts down for the winter, the greens are fenced off to protect them from the foraging elk. Sulphur Mountain, Tunnel Mountain, and Mount Rundle tower on every side. The Bow and Spray rivers slash through the course in the spring, calming to a resolute flow as the days warm and lengthen.

When the new nine and clubhouse were added, the Thompson course was reconfigured so that all the nines could begin in the same location. The current Rundle nine is comprised of the 5th through the 13th holes of the original course. The Sulphur nine are holes numbers 1 through 4 and the 14th through the 18th. The new holes are called the Tunnel nine.

The 4th hole on the Rundle, called the Cauldron, is the hole that everyone takes with them to the grave. You emerge from the woods onto an elevated tee to see a

The 9th on the Rundle runs along the Bow River toward the striking Banff Springs Hotel.

green 171 yards away across a glacial lake painted on a canvas of mountains. If it's not be the prettiest hole in the world, it's definitely on the front nine.

Though the 4th is world famous, the 2nd hole on the Rundle shouldn't be overlooked. It's a 174-yarder uphill across a huge valley to a big green set against a giant mountain backdrop—almost the opposite of the Cauldron. With the altitude (right around a mile above sea level and about a one club difference) and the setting, it's hard to pull the right club out of the bag.

The 1st hole on the Sulphur is called Little Bow, a 230-yard par three with water diverted from the river running up the entire right hand side. Sulphur number 3, Big Bow, is the very difficult 420-yard, par four companion. The Bow River is on the right as the hole closes in on the green with a big bunker left and about 30 feet in between them.

Sulphur number 5 is the old 18th, and it plays directly toward the majestic hotel modelled after a Scottish baronial castle. There are also 26 bunkers to get your attention. The 6th, the old number 1, plays 411 yards across the Spray River with Mount Rundle towering over the entire hole. The 9th on the Sulphur has proven itself to be a fine finishing hole. It's a 578-yard, dogleg right par five with out of bounds on the right. The big hitters can cut the corner across trees and mountain—a carry of about 240—and reach the green in two. But out here, why hurry?

The Canadian Rockies seem to rise straight up from the edges of the fairway.

Barton Creek
Texas

If Ben Crenshaw plays there, that's good enough for me. Period. Crenshaw knows golf. And Barton Creek Conference Resort and CC just happens to be his home course. It also happens to be the new home of the Legends of Golf—that stroke of genius that gave birth to the PGA Senior Tour. The wily, over-the-hill gang might be too tactful to say Barton Creek is the best course they play, but I'd bet the ranch they'd put it in their top two.

Opened in 1986, this Tom Fazio masterpiece is set in the Texas Hill Country outside Austin, one of the prettiest parts of the state, filled with creeks, caves, and waterfalls. And Fazio uses them all to great advantage at Barton Creek.

Fazio's course plays 6,956 yards from the tip of the gold tees. A goodly number of the holes play downhill, cutting the distance somewhat but not the challenge. The 1st, for example, plays downhill, but at 460 it's a monster no matter how you look at it.

The 5th is a superb five par of 611 with a double fairway and water fronting the green. The 7th is a very difficult 442-yard dogleg left with a large bunker guarding the corner. The 8th is a par five of just 494 yards, but water guards the left and woods and cliffs the right. The green is a very scary target in two. The 9th is the first of Barton Creek's most spectacular holes. It's a 175-yarder over pure Texas wilderness to a green guarded by a waterfall—just a lovely, lovely hole.

The 418-yard 10th drops over 100 feet from the tee to the fairway. There's a highly hook-receptive lake on the left. The 12th is the hardest 270-yard par four you'll ever play. The 13th is a Texas-size four par of 477. It's been unlucky for a lot of folks. The 15th is a brilliant 527 yard par five. There are fairway bunkers that need to be avoided to even consider getting home in two but the dropoff on the left down to the river is the real danger.

The 16th is a downhill 420-yarder that is simply one of the prettiest holes in the state of Texas. The green is fronted by a creek and a series of waterfalls. And the 18th is a spectacular 546-yard par five with a cave guarding the fairway and what seems like a limestone quarry protecting the green on your uphill approach.

A creek and stone wall make for a tricky short iron approach on the long 5th, a par five of over 600 yards.

One of the Texas Hill Country's waterfalls cascades alongside the gorgeous 16th, a 420-yard, downhill par four.

Bethpage Black
New York

Anyone who loves traditional golf will fall in love with Bethpage Black. It holds a position of honor in this compendium because it's the only A.W. Tillinghast course and was, in fact, his last. Tillinghast, of course, was the unconventional, even profligate, genius of golf course architecture who created such masterworks as Winged Foot, San Francisco Golf Club, Baltusrol, and Quaker Ridge.

Bethpage Black is all the more unusual because it's in a state park, part of a 90-hole golf complex that was built during the Great Depression as a WPA project. At one time over 1,800 people were employed at Bethpage State Park in various construction projects. Tillinghast designed three of the Bethpage courses, one of which was partially lost when the fifth, or Yellow, course was built in 1958.

He concluded his work on the stunning and difficult Black in 1936.

You should know from the start that the Black Course from the championship tees is not for the timid. It plays 7,065 yards to a par of 71, mostly through dense woods. There are no carts on Bethpage Black—yet another reason to love it. You walk and carry your bag or take a pull cart. What greater pleasure can a golfer enjoy than to make a putt for birdie on a sloping, slick saucer-shaped Tillinghast green, shoulder his bag, and walk a few yards through a wooded tunnel to emerge at the next tee? An optimistic scenario, to be sure, because birdies are an endangered species on the Black.

One of Bethpage Black's sternest holes is the 430-yard,

dogleg right par four 1st. There's a big tree at the corner of the dogleg and very few people can fly it. Play this hole as designed.

The 446-yard 5th is a Tillinghast classic. From an elevated tee you must drive the ball over the huge fairway bunker (which is no mean feat) and then play a long iron to an elevated green with an enormous bunker on the left. The 6th is a cutie. You can fly the fairway bunkers on this 404-yard dogleg left and successfully cut the corner, but if you do, you're left with a tough downhill lie.

The 8th is a 195-yarder downhill par three with a pond in front. Watch out for the second pond, though, left of the green. You can't see it from the tee.

The 12th is a man-size 480-yard par four that requires another one of those tremendous carries over bunkers to reach the fairway. The 15th is 438 yards with a second shot that plays dramatically uphill. Miss right and you can roll down the hill and out of bounds. Miss left and you're above the green with a testy little pitch shot. The 16th is another killer four par. It's 466 yards with deep fescue left and right. The drive is downhill and, once again, you're tempted to cut the corner. If you don't clear the tall fescue, though, a lost ball is a good chance, and even if you find it you're going to be harvesting some wheat.

Tillinghast lets you finish strong. At the 18th you can fly the trouble and play a short iron into the green. Consider it a consolation birdie from one of America's master builders.

Bunkers front the green on the treacherous 6th. The trouble is finding a level spot in the fairway for the approach.

There is only the narrowest of openings to the 12th green, a gigantic par four of 480 yards.

Blackwolf Run
Wisconsin

This hole is called "Gotcha"—uphill and 461 yards. It's the first of several punishingly long par fours.

The second hole is called "Burial Mounds", which you can see on the left. You're dead if you're on them.

Blackwolf Run is one of those very rare places that takes you completely by surprise. North of Sheboygan in the village of Kohler, Wisconsin, Pete Dye (with a great deal of help from the Sheboygan River) has created one of the great golfing masterpieces to be found anywhere in the Midwest.

Blackwolf Run is built on a breathtakingly beautiful piece of land formed by glacial runoff and the meandering river adjacent to the 600-acre River Wildlife game preserve. Centuries ago this land was prime hunting ground for the native tribes that roamed between what is now Milwaukee and Green Bay. Thanks to Dye, it's prime hunting ground for golfers today.

The River Course is 6,991 yards from the back tees. From the 1st hole on, it asks no quarter and gives none. The opening hole has the Sheboygan River along the length of the left side. One way or another, the river comes into play on over half the holes. After the short 2nd, a dramatic par four guarded by mounds and deep grasses, one of the hardest holes on the golf course looms ahead. The 461-yard, par four 3rd—dubbed "Gotcha"— should be regarded as a par four and one half, the first of three such monsters. It's a dogleg right, slightly uphill. There's a chasm and large bunker threatening the tee shot on the right. A tee ball placed on the left side of the fairway will roll back toward the middle. A giant bunker threatens the entire right side of the hole, so hang it out to the left. Remember, bogey is a good score here.

After Dye's diabolical opening holes, the 4th is a cute three par of 195 yards with a pond on the entire right side. Everything kicks right, too. This is no place to be overly bold. The 5th tee offers one of the most beautiful views of the course, with the river running off on the right-hand side.

continued

The par three 4th requires nothing less than perfection with mounds and bunkers on the left and water all the way up the right side.

17

Down in the valley with the Sheboygan River, the 10th has water on the right and bunkers just about everywhere else.

Blackwolf Run, continued

The 9th through 13th holes are all in the valley along the Sheboygan River. They are the kind of golf holes that are so beautiful you almost begin to forget how hard they are. Don't worry, Dye brings you around with the 465-yard 12th, called "Long Lagoon"—Monster Number 2. It takes a big drive to carry the lagoon and the bunker beyond it. There is some room to the right for the faint of heart. The river is on the right for the very long second shot.

The 16th is a teaser par five of 560 yards. The perfect drive will catch the hill and roll out where you might be tempted to go for the green in two shots. Don't. Play short of the green (and the river), pitch up, and try to make your four that way. And just in case you haven't come across enough strong par fours for one day, there's a 469-yard, dogleg left par four 18th to finish. That's Monster Number 3. Black-wolf Run is a difficult golf course but one you could never tire of looking at—or playing.

The Boulders
Arizona

You simply have to love a place that's called Carefree. And it would be difficult not to love the Boulders, tucked away among the balancing rocks and saguaro cactus of the high Sonoran desert north of Scottsdale. Carefree has become something of a hideaway for the rich and famous. It also happens to be the hideaway of one the world's great golf resorts.

Jay Morrish was commissioned by Laurance Rockefeller to design the three existing nines—the Lake, Boulders, and Saguaro—which were completed in 1985. Previously, the championship configuration was Lake/Boulders. But the addition of another nine holes, also by Morrish, has allowed the creation of two separate courses. The one featured here is the Saguaro, comprised of the current Lake and Saguaro nines. The other is the Boulders course, combining the current Boulders nine plus the new nine.

Once an associate in Jack Nicklaus' golf course design company, Morrish has partnered with Tom Weiskopf on nearby Troon North and the TPC at Scottsdale, both of which appear in this book. It would be absurd to say that any desert golf course looks natural, regardless of the number of javelinas (a kind of wild boar), coyotes, or two-hundred-year-old saguaros it has. Still, Morrish has a gentle touch in his golf courses, and it's evident in all the holes at the Boulders. Desert golf, with wide expanses of undisturbed terrain, is by definition "target" golf. Morrish is fastidious in his preservation of the desert, yet he attempts to make the course reasonably playable. It's a tough note to hit, but it resonates at the Boulders.

Be advised, the Lake is a very long nine holes of golf. It begins with a 451-yard, slightly uphill par four followed by the 445-yard, dogleg right 2nd. The drive needs to be played to the right of the boulder in the fairway, and there's a deep pot bunker to the right of the green. Just in case you hadn't had enough of long par fours, Morrish gives you the 457-

continued

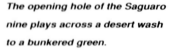

The opening hole of the Saguaro nine plays across a desert wash to a bunkered green.

The fairways at The Boulders are like green ribbons in the Sonoran desert. Don't be surprised if you see the occasional coyote.

Tall Saguaro cacti stand like sentinels near the tee on the 9th hole. You needn't play as far to the right as it appears.

The Boulders, continued

yard 4th. Your second shot must carry a wash.

The Saguaro is, thankfully, a good deal shorter than the Lake, but it plays tighter, too. It also might be the prettiest of the three original nines. The 513-yard, par five opening hole has two carries over desert wash. It's reachable if you drive it in the fairway. The 3rd hole is a 548-yard stunner. Drive it at the last fairway bunker on this dogleg left. There's a creek in front of the green, a lake, and pot bunker left. Play it safe here. The 5th is the most challenging of Saguaro's four pars. The drive must find the right center of the fairway or an ironwood tree will prevent a clean shot at this well-bunkered, sloped green. The 9th is a beautiful hole. Framed in saguaro cactus, you play to a narrow green with bunkers behind and right.

It's a perfect spot to finish as the golden, dusty light sweeps over the desert and the coyotes take over.

Boyne Highlands
Michigan

Marsh, bunkers and a distinct ridge in the green make the Heather's 173-yard 6th hole a challenge.

Mist floats off the cool ponds on many Northern Michigan mornings.

There's nothing quite like hearing the thwack of club and ball echo down a fairway burrowed like a cave through a virgin forest of oak and maple. It's the perfect sound of the game, an auditory confirmation of precise execution. The flight of the ball becomes almost superfluous. The sound has told you whether it will be close or not. Your eyes merely confirm what you already know.

The Heather Course at Boyne Highlands is such a place, made all the more pleasurable because the test of golf is as crisp and clean as a well-struck iron. The Heather has been the focus of one of golf's most successful reconstruction projects.

Robert Trent Jones introduced the Heather to rave reviews in 1971. After a second course, the Moor, was completed, the two courses were intermingled, making it impossible to play the Jones layout in one 18-hole round. The result wasn't bad but it wasn't the original masterpiece, either. The good news is the full Heather has been restored. Now you play it the way Jones intended.

From the very back tees, the Heather is a big golf course playing 7,210 yards and usually without a lot of roll. Choose your tees carefully. The challenge begins at the 437-yard 3rd, a very difficult driving hole. Aim at the pine tree dead ahead and fade it just a little. There's water short and left of the green. The 4th is a 215-yard par three to a wide green sloped back to front. The 5th is a sweeping dogleg left par five of 563 yards. There's a lake on the left threatening every shot. Number 6 is a par three of 173 yards to a green that has a pronounced ridge in the middle, separating left and right. The 7th is a position par four. Don't drive it through the fairway into the bunker on this dogleg left. Number 8 is a monster four par of 449 yards. The drive must find the fairway between bunkers left and water right. Finish up the outward half with a 592-yard par five. Take your second shot over the marsh on the left, and cut off as much of the dogleg as you can.

There aren't many breathers on the back. Try to pick up a shot on the 501-yard, par five 15th. Take your drive over the trees on the left if you dare. If you want to know what the back nine has in store for you, check out the par fours—the 421-yard 10th (a well-bunkered green); the 431-yard 13th (tough just to reach the dogleg); the 462-yard 14th (to a shallow green no less!); the 423-yard 17th (another big hit to reach the dogleg and a formidable ridge in the green); and the 468-yard 18th to a double-sloped green with water in front.

Now put your feet up by the fire in the chalet. You've earned the rest.

Breckenridge
Colorado

A mountain stream, complete with beaver ponds, flanks the very difficult 580-yard par five 12th.

The Breckenridge Golf Club is a stunning Rocky Mountain course with a past as checkered as the old mining towns that surround it. Periods of boom and bust are nothing new to these tiny Colorado communities whose fortunes soared well over a hundred years ago with silver and dried up as soon as the veins tapped out. Powdery snow and skiers with deep pockets brought the good times back—until the real estate crash. And so it goes.

The course has suffered its share of ups and downs. Work began in 1982, and because of the short growing season at 9,300 feet above sea level it wasn't until 1985 that nine holes were ready to open. It became clear almost immediately that there were drainage problems with the greens and they wouldn't withstand any significant amount of play. The course was closed, and all 18 greens were reconstructed. It's still a matter of dispute as to who was responsible for the inadequate original construction. Nonetheless, the new, improved and complete Breckenridge Golf Club opened for play in 1987.

The fact that Breckenridge had to be rebuilt before it even opened should not deceive anyone. This is a wonderful golf course in a breathtaking (in more ways than one) setting. Mountains from four different ranges—the Ten Mile, the Gore, the Williams Fork, and the Front—surround you. Deer and elk come out in the evenings. Hawks circle in the daytime looking for a light repast hiding among the wildflowers. A series of beaver ponds stairstep down the 12th. The holes play over wetlands, through forests, and in open prairie. It's a treat for the senses.

But not for the scoring average. This is a very difficult golf course. From the back tees it's 7,279 yards. Though situated at 9,300 feet, there's also a lot of water and a lot of wilderness out there. Think of it as a tight 7,000 yards.

The front nine has a particularly difficult finish, with the 7th hole playing 224 yards to a green guarded in front by a creek, followed by two colossal prairie par fours, the 461-yard 8th and the 473-yard 9th. A stream flows up the entire right side of the 8th to cross the fairway in front of the green.

The 580-yard 12th is one of the truly magnificent holes on the course. There's creek on both sides (though the left much more in play) and a fairway bunker off the tee. On your second you must avoid the ponds on the right, and your third shot must carry the water with a greenside bunker back right. Every bit as hard as it is beautiful.

The finish on the back nine is not quite as brutal as the front. The 16th is a three par of 177 yards with a horseshoe of sand around the front and sides of the green. The tee shot on the 416-yard 17th must carry a trio of cross bunkers set diagonally in the fairway. And the 423-yard 18th is a second-shot hole to a green protected by a lake and bunkers.

The Ten Mile Range is just one of four mountain backdrops at Breckenridge. The Gore, Williams Fork and Front Ranges are also all in view.

The Broadmoor
Colorado

There's nothing quite like the look on a flat-lander's face after his first encounter with mountain golf. It's a different game up there, where the air is thin and ball seems to fly forever. There's more to it than just learning how to throttle down on your club selection, though. It's the quizzical look on a player's face after watching a putt he was sure was going to break six inches right sweep a foot to the left instead.

Nowhere is mountain golf played with more style than at The Broadmoor in Colorado Springs, at the base of the Rocky Mountains. Cheyenne Mountain—with its full complement of military antennae— looms behind the hotel. The Will Rogers Memorial clings to a

precipice above the South Course, an Arnold Palmer/Ed Seay design that has hosted the USGA Women's Amateur.

Donald Ross transformed this winter playground when he designed the first 18 holes in 1918. From 1950 to 1964, Robert Trent Jones added an additional 18 holes, and the Jones and Ross layouts have been combined to make Broadmoor's East and West courses.

The East is Broadmoor's crown jewel. The Ross holes are Numbers 1 through 3 as well as 13 through 18, everything on the hotel side of Cheyenne Mountain Boulevard. Jones provides everything across the road, numbers 4 through 12.

The East's most famous hole is the 15th, the original 18th. It was there that Jack Nicklaus made a birdie three on this 421 par four over water to defeat Charlie Coe 1 up in the 36-hole final for the US Amateur Championship of 1959—Nicklaus' first major victory.

Uniquely, the East Course seems to hang together as a unified whole despite the fact that half the holes were Ross creations and the other half Jones designs. The fairways are relatively wide. The greens are large and desperately confusing. The land is not heavily wooded, just irritatingly populated with enough pines to thwart the best-laid plans.

Remember, the altitude at the Broadmoor is 6,000 feet. As a result, the 6,937-yard East plays much shorter than the card would lead you to believe. Figure a club and a half to two clubs for the longer shots, one club for the short irons. As for ye olde flat stick—everything breaks away from the Will Rogers Memorial unless there's water, then it breaks in that direction.

The 6th, 7th, and 10th are the most severe tests among the Jones-created holes. The 6th is a dogleg left 544-yard, dogleg left par five. It's possible to get home in two, but you have to carry a lake to do it. The 7th and 10th holes are big four pars, the former a 471-yard dogleg left and the latter a 488-yard dogleg right.

The Ross finish has some classic holes. The 14th is a puny little 619-yard par five. The 15th is, well, only historic. The 16th is a short one-shot hole of 165 yards, but woe to those who miss the green. The 18th is a top-notch finishing par five of 573 yards to a green guarded in front by water.

The fairway dips and rolls toward the 11th green, one of the Robert Trent Jones holes on the East Course.

The Broadmoor Hotel and the Rockies tower behind the 13th, a Donald Ross par three of 182 yards surrounded with bunkers.

Cantigny

Illinois

The Dick Tracy bunker livens up the 18th hole, a 365-yard par four with water on both sides and behind the green.

educational area. Open on the grounds at Cantigny are the ornate McCormick mansion frequently used for indoor concerts, ten acres of gardens designed by Franz Lipp, 27 holes of golf, and the official museum of the United States Army's First Division.

Cantigny is also a 6,709-yard masterpiece among the oaks and ash, woven between lakes and streams. The original 18 hole course (a supplemental nine has been added) was designed by Roger Packard, something of a Midwestern celebrity in golf course architecture, and opened in 1989.

Among the challenges on the front nine is the 2nd, a 539-yard par five with a feeder stream running up the right side. It weaves across the fairway and then back again. To reach the green in two shots you have to carry the water not once but twice while aiming at a green bunkered in front with another small lake behind. The lay up is no picnic either—it must be played to the little section of fairway cut off by the meandering stream. The 3rd hole is 200 yards over a lake and huge bunker area. The horse topiary you see at the tee is called "Silverwings" and is the burial site of fourteen of McCormick's horses killed in a stable fire. The 8th plays 165 yards to a green completely surrounded by water.

On the back the 11th is a double-dogleg par five of 556 yards. The drive is between water

Cantigny was the name of the estate of Robert R. McCormick, editor and publisher of the *Chicago Tribune* from 1911 to 1955. He named it after a small French village that was the site the United States Army's first offensive of World War I. McCormick served in France as an artillery battalion commander in the Army's First Division, better known as the Big Red One. His will requested that after his death a portion of his estate, comprising approximately 500 acres, be kept as a public recreational and

"Silverwings" marks the burial site of 14 horses McCormick lost in a stable fire.

right and a bunker on the left. The second shot should carry well beyond a neck between two lakes to a position guarded by a fairway bunker on the left. The hole then turns back left to the green bunkered on the left. A definite three-shot hole.

The 13th is a splendid par three of 191 yards over water. The lake on the left and bunker on the right make the entrance to the green seem very narrow.

The drive on the 516-yard 14th has got to find a safe spot away from a huge expanse of fairway bunkers. The hole doglegs right into another sea of sand.

Cantigny's 18th plays 365 yards with water on the right and a fairway bunker shaped like Dick Tracy about 260 yards out on the right. The green has water left, right, and behind.

Water and woods team to make Cantigny, built on the former estate of Robert R. McCormick, narrow and tough.

Carambola
Virgin Islands

At 477 yards, the 13th looms as a thunderously difficult par four. Don't let your long second shot get away to the right.

Like many of the Caribbean Islands, St. Croix in the U.S. Virgins can be a disturbing combination of paradise and poverty. It was made even more so when Hurricane Hugo decimated this idyllic island in 1989. The storm wrecked unimaginable violence. The tourist industry, the island's lifeblood, was virtually destroyed.

One of the most severely damaged of St. Croix' resorts was Carambola Beach, located on the north shore along Davis Bay. It took over a year for the hotel to reopen. Major renovations were also undertaken on the splendid Robert Trent Jones course laid out in the valley a short distance inland from the ocean. All eighteen greens were rebuilt. New white sand was shipped to the island to refill all the bunkers. The result has been the reclamation of one of the greatest golf courses in the tropics.

Carambola Beach Golf Club lies in the valley between two ridges of mountains in the western section of St. Croix. High on the forested hills you can see the conical rock remnants of the windmills used in grinding sugar cane for the island's colonial plantations. Not far away there's a dense rain forest. Back in the mountains is a sheer cliff, stone quarry, and winding paths passable only by jeep or on horseback. The golf course is serene in comparison. It rolls gently through palms and bougainvillea. When it was constructed in 1966, Jones referred to it as "the loveliest course I ever built."

It's also a terrific test of golf. The front nine is short and quite strategic. Typical are the 3rd, barely 300 yards but very tight with the green fit snugly into a horseshoe of water, and the 4th, a picturesque dogleg right par five of just 458 yards. If you keep your tee ball left center and

It takes a huge drive just to reach the corner on the dogleg left 18th. From there it's all uphill on this 476-yard finishing hole.

reach the dogleg you can hit the green in two. The second will be uphill, over a stream to a green protected by deep bunkers on the left.

The back nine is big, however. The 13th is the first of two enormous par fours. It's 477 yards, dogleg right with a downhill second. Don't lose that second shot right. There's water over there. The 15th is a three-shot hole all the way. Slightly uphill, it plays every bit of its 593 yards

to a heavily bunkered green.

The final two holes are marvelous. The 17th is 185 across a pond—more of a ravine these days—to a wide green bunkered behind. The 18th is prodigious. The drive is out of a chute across the extension of the aforementioned watery ravine. The 476-yard hole doglegs left and it takes a tremendous blow just to reach the corner. From there it's all uphill to the clubhouse.

The target on the par three 5th can seem mighty small. It's 179 yards all carry across a pond with bunkers left and right.

Casa de Campo
Dominican Republic

Casa de Campo is the Cypress Point of the Caribbean. It's also the only golf course I know where you can land an airplane on one hole and then play it the same day.

Pete Dye's magnificent layout on the southeastern coast of the Dominican Republic is most easily reached by puddle-jumper from Puerto Rico. It's a 30-minute flight from San Juan to the airport at La Romana, and the landing strip is adjacent the resort. In fact, your tee shot on the 440-yard, uphill 18th is played across the runway, lending an entirely new meaning to the golfer's credo "Tee it high and let it fly."

Built almost entirely by hand, or at least in a manner that the giant earth-moving architects of North America would consider primitive, Casa de Campo's first 18 holes opened in 1971 as the Campo de Golf Cajuiles, the latter

continued

The wind plays havoc on the 16th, a 185-yard par three along the rocky edge of the Caribbean.

This is the view from Chez Dye on the 7th.

word being Spanish for "cashew," a reference to the many such trees on the grounds. The name was eventually changed: With six holes playing along the rocky and windy Caribbean coast, somehow "cashew" was too benign a term for the course. Golfers had already come to respect and even fear these holes. Dye's course was quickly redubbed "Teeth of the Dog" and has been known that way ever since.

The Dog does, indeed, bite. The 5th is the first of the string of three front nine holes with the Caribbean on the left. It's just 155 yards, but the tiny green is protected by sea, rocks, a guardian tree, flotsam and jetsam. Naturally, the wind can turn club selection on this hole into something resembling a voodoo ritual.

The 6th is brutal. From the back tees, it's 449 yards with the rocks and oblivion all along the left. Speaking of brutal, the 7th is 225 yards from the championship tees. If you thought club selection was an odious chore on the 5th, try it here. One thing about Teeth of the Dog, though, while the 6th and 7th are enormously difficult from the championship tees, from the membership markers they play a very comfortable 387 and 120, fully 167 yards shorter. Wave to Dye as you play the 7th. That's his thatched-roof bungalow overlooking the green and the sea. He's built a lot of golf courses since 1971, but he returns to this one.

The beauties of the back nine are the 15th, 16th, and 17th holes along the sea. Each seems to have its green perched precariously above the water, walled off from the crashing waves. The championship tees are little more than launching pads in the midst of the blue Caribbean.

The tiny 5th green is a tough target to hit or hold. The tree makes the approach extremely narrow.

The 15th is 384 and a difficult fairway to hit. The 16th is 185 and like the three pars on the front, the wind makes the hole. The 17th is a very difficult par four of 435 yards. Sea up the right, trees up the left—beautiful but daunting.

The 440-yard 18th—with an uphill second shot to a well-bunkered green with a hazard guarding the left—is a demanding finish. And watch out for that Piper Cub.

The surf isn't the only hazard on the very difficult 420-yard 15th, just the toughest one. Getting the ball in the fairway is a challenge.

Cog Hill
Illinois

The Chicago environs is as rich in golf tradition as any metropolitan area in the country. US Opens and PGA Championships make frequent stops there. Decades ago the now extinct Tam O'Shanter was one of the fledgling PGA Tour's glamour stops. The Western Open—once a traveling tournament that rivaled the national Open in importance and now a PGA Tour annual event—is as permanent a Chicago-area fixture as the Cubs. The Western's latest move has been from Butler National to Cog Hill's Number 4 course, better known as Dubsdread.

It's a particularly fitting move because it underscores the importance of public golf in Chicago's tradition. Cog Hill is owned by Joe Jemsek, who has been bringing high-caliber public golf to Chicago since buying the St. Andrews Golf Club in 1939. His dedication to the proposition that this silly pastime is for everyone has earned him honors from virtually every organization in the game, from the National Golf Foundation to his own Chicago District. Today Jemsek's open-to-all empire includes nine

The sun rises at the dogleg of the 7th, a short par four with an amoeba-shaped green.

courses at five different locations. And none is better than his Dubsdread.

Jemsek acquired Cog Hill in 1951, but it wasn't until the 1964 opening of the Joe Lee-designed Number 4 course, a 6,992-yard par 72 that immediately acquired the nickname "Dubsdread," that Cog Hill earned a measure of national recognition. So highly regarded, it was quickly selected as the site of the 1970 US Public Links Championship.

Dubsdread opens with a "little" dogleg left par four of 449 yards to a double-tiered green guarded by four bunkers aligned along the front and sides. Narrow takes on a whole new meaning at the 4th. Two irritating little water hazards are in the right and left rough about 220 out from the tee. Past them, the fairway narrows down even more with bunkers and trees. Short of the hazards, you still have 150 yards or so into a tiny, completely bunkered green. Number 9 is 576 yards of "thread the needle."

To make your score, you need to get off to a good start on the back. The 10th is a short four par that can be challenged. The 11th is a fairly open par five of 517 yards, and the 12th is a testy 197-yarder to another tiered green. After that it's back to the salt mines (or perhaps stock yards would be more apt) at the 13th, with trees right, bunkers left, and a very narrow target up ahead. The 14th is a simply gorgeous 197-yard par three to a green surrounded by sand. And the 18th is 439 yards, bunkers left and right off the tee, water left of the green and bunkers right.

It's tough to get to the 18th green from this fairway bunker. And there's water behind that willow.

The 197-yard 14th is literally surrounded by bunkers. The hole plays slightly downhill and there's plenty of green to work with.

Concord
New York

The Concord Resort Hotel can be found among the woodland and rolling foothills of New York's Catskill Mountains. The Monster, as it has come to be known, was built in 1963 by Joe Finger. From its championship markers the course measures 7,471 yards (although it *can* play at over 7,900 yards). Plan on wearing out those long irons and fairway woods.

If you're not striking the ball well, the sheer magnitude of the Monster likely will be overwhelming. It's precisely when your game is "on" that the full genius of the course reveals itself and, in the case of most of us, unmasks our frauds and deficiencies.

Several cases in point: The 4th hole is a giant par five of 610 yards. The drive is played uphill with water hidden on the left, unseen from the tee. From about 200 yards in, the hazard cuts diagonally across the fairway, left to right, creating a go or no-go dilemma for the second shot. You can choose to fly the hazard on the left for a shorter club to the green or lay up to the right.

The Monster is cut through a forest in the Catskills. It can play as long as 7,900 yards but who would want to?

The 15th hole is a dogleg left of 481 yards. The tee shot must find the right side of the fairway. There's a fairway bunker about 240 out from the tee, which is your target line. The fairway slopes left so anything that doesn't stay on the flat will roll left and be blocked by trees on the second shot. Even if you're positioned perfectly, it's still a long, long way.

The 17th hole is the course's namesake. It's a 420-yard par four with an unusual configuration of water hazards in the fairway. On the left side there's water short, fairway long. On the right side, it's fairway short, water long. It's 270 yards from the championship tees to clear the water on the left. Gamble left for the easier second shot. Play it safe right but be faced with a killer second.

The 18th is a meager 476 yards. If you don't hop all over your tee ball, you simply can't get there in two shots. The green is 55 yards deep.

By the time the Monster has finished with you, if that "A" game still rates a "B-" you've done a fine day's work.

It takes nothing less than two perfectly struck shots to get home on the 484-yard 18th.

Desert Dunes
California

Desert Dunes Golf Club is one of those rare blends of an exceptional piece of ground and an exceptional piece of golf course architecture. Robert Trent Jones Jr. took a patch of desert and mesquite outside of Palm Springs and fashioned one of the most strikingly beautiful and playable courses in the Coachilla Valley.

The first three holes are prelude to the desert landscape that follows. Beginning with the 4th hole the stark terrain becomes an ever-present hazard.

The tee ball on this 406-yard dogleg left par four must avoid the desert mounds on the right. The ideal shot is at the fairway bunker. The 5th is a gorgeous 176-yard par three with desert and deep bunkers all around. The short 6th and 7th holes are incredibly tight par fours. Be con-tent to keep the ball in play here and thread the needle through the mounds of mesquite. Like so many of the holes at Desert Dunes, birdie is a possibility but so is triple-bogey. The 7th green, at the end of a hooked fair-way, is protected by water behind. That pond serves as the main hazard on the right of the 181-yard 8th.

The 9th is a tough 546-yard five par with desert hills on the right and a long fairway bunker (separating the 9th and 18th fairways) on the left. At one narrow point the bunker is traversed by an imitation of the Swilcan Bridge. The 9th and 18th holes form a double green, though one could hardly call it a "common" green. They are huge putting surfaces with a giant swale and bunker in between.

The 10th and 11th holes are carved from a tamarisk forest and duplicate the challenge of the short 6th and 7th—back-to-back par fours where you must be concerned primarily with putting the ball in play. Anything in the trees is virtually unplayable. You'll be lucky if you can punch it back to the fairway.

Desert Dunes' final six holes are as

continued

The 17th is a 192-yard par three guarded by mounds, deep bunkers and desert.

Desert Dunes, continued

demanding as they are stunning. The 13th is a 586-yard par five that features a particularly dangerous tee shot. The 192-yard 14th is played to a well-bunkered green. The 15th and 16th are my favorites. The tee shot on the 431-yard 15th is played short of a fairway bunker and patch of mesquite that serves as a cross hazard. The 16th, a 530-yard par five, plays to a green guarded by a pond that serves as a perfect reflecting pool for the mountain vista behind.

The finish includes another fine par three, the 192-yard 17th and the very difficult 443-yard 18th. It's great golf in a majestic setting.

The pond by the 16th makes a peaceful reflecting pool for the mountains beyond Palm Springs.

The 8th is a demanding par three with water right and a bunker left. The green in the distance is the 7th, a very narrow 398-yard par four.

Desert Inn
Nevada

The 173-yard 16th has water and bunkers at every turn. Be sure to avoid the tiny pot bunker on the right.

If you're left of the 7th green, you're swimming. Always one of the toughest one-shot holes on the PGA Tour.

Not many people journey to Las Vegas to play golf. Considering this, it's quite a surprise to find a course like the Desert Inn CC there. The Desert Inn has been the home, or one of the homes, of a PGA Tour event since the Tournament of Champions came to "the Strip" in 1953 and first prize was paid off in a wheelbarrow full of silver dollars. The winners have included folks like Sam Snead, Gene Littler, Arnold Palmer, and Jack Nicklaus.

The Desert Inn has the rare distinction of hosting both a regular PGA Tour and a Senior PGA Tour tournament—the young limberbacks play the Las Vegas Invitational, a five-day marathon conducted on three different layouts, and the older gentlemen have the Las Vegas Senior Classic there. Located in the middle of the city's famed Strip, this peaceful, tree-lined course is like a desert oasis. It's long—stretching out to 7,111 yards from the back tees—and very cleverly bunkered.

The 7th is the DI's signature hole. Year in and year out it ranks as one of the toughest short holes on the PGA Tour. It's 205 yards to a V-shaped green guarded by water (and a stone wall) on the left and bunkers right and behind. It's natural to play away from the pond but if you're too far right that bunker shot back toward the water is no walk in the park.

The front nine finishes off with two long, hard par fours—the 442-yard 8th and the 432-yard 9th. Surviving this stretch—the 7th, 8th, and 9th—is the key to any round at Desert Inn. And, of course, if you don't survive them there's always the option of a stiff bracer at the turn.

The 10th parallels the opening hole and likely will give you a solid run at birdie. The 11th can be a difficult par three because of its length, but from this point on, anyone who is on their game should have some birdie opportunities. In virtually every instance, though, positioning of the tee ball is the crucial shot.

The 512-yard 15th yields its fair share of birdies, but guard against going right. The 16th is a picturesque 173-yarder with some devilish pot bunkers. The 17th is only 395 yards but requires a precise drive and crisp second. The 18th is a tough, dogleg right of 432 yards. A good final hole, you better have your score made before you get here.

Doral
Florida

It's in Florida but it's no where near the beach. It's on the direct glide path into Miami International Airport, and a constant stream of jets roar overhead. And a little over thirty years ago, it was a useless piece of swampland. So what have we got here? Only one of the best golf courses east of the Mississippi—Doral's Blue Monster.

The Blue was built in 1960 by Dick Wilson for Alfred Kaskel, who envisioned a great golf resort on the swampy alligator-infested outskirts of Miami. Two years later Kaskel bought a date on the PGA Tour by offering double the prize money of any other professional event in Florida and the Monster was introduced to the public and the pros alike. Ever since it has been a favorite of both.

Courses are constantly being evaluated on the basis of the star quality of the players who have won there. Here are Doral's credentials: Jack Nicklaus, twice; Billy Casper, twice; Doug Sanders, twice; Ray Floyd, twice; Andy Bean, three times; Mark McCumber, twice; Lee Trevino; Hubert Green; Tom Weiskopf; Tom Kite; Lanny Wadkins; Ben Crenshaw; Greg Norman. Tidy little group, isn't it?

The 3rd is where the Monster rears its lush, green head. It's a 402-yard par four with water all along on the right, trees left. The 4th is 225 yards over water to a sloped green protected by bunkers on both sides. The 8th is one of my favorites, a classic 528-yard par five. The hole plays into a prevailing wind, and the green is guarded by water front, right, and behind, so reaching it in two shots is a risky proposition.

Water guards the entire left side of the par five 10th hole, so it's best to favor the right side of the fairway—making this hole play every inch of its 543 yards. The 11th is a clever little par four of just 351

continued

It can be touchy trying to hit the 8th green where water wraps around this wonderful 528-yard par five.

The Blue Monster's 437-yard 18th is acknowledged to be one of the greatest finishing holes in golf. Very difficult driving hole. Very difficult second.

Doral, continued

yards with a huge bunker area in the middle of the fairway. Off the tee you can play left, right, or lay up short.

The 12th and 13th holes are the Monster's backbone. The 608-yard 12th is one of the great three-shot par fives anywhere in the world. And the 13th is a par three of just 246 yards. Most players don't see the green here until their second shot.

If the 12th and 13th are the backbone, the 17th and 18th are the muscle. So much is made of the final hole that the tricky 17th is frequently forgotten. A 426-yard dogleg right with bunkers on both sides of the landing area, it plays to a triple-level green that is over 60 yards in length.

And, of course, there is the 18th, which is without doubt one of the great final holes in the world. Only Ben Crenshaw has birdied the 437-yard 18th to win. With water all along the left and trees on the right, the drive must be perfect. The green is set at an angle for the second shot. The short pin position is often tougher than the back one. With the shorter approach iron anything pulled a bit can find the water. And you may have already visited it once with the driver. It's a par four and a half, but a great one.

Above the 7th fairway you can see all the elements that make Doral so difficult.

The 13th is such a long par three that many people simply can't reach it.

Edgewood Tahoe
Nevada

Tom Fazio is unquestionably one of the best modern golf course architects. He has been recognized by his peers and acknowledged by the players. But before Tom there was his uncle, George Fazio, PGA Tour player and golf course architect. Tom got his training working with George—whose most famous creations are Jupiter Hills in Florida and Edgewood Tahoe in Nevada, which has the horrible misfortune of being built on the banks of the world's greatest reflecting pool, Lake Tahoe.

What a pity to have to tee it up right there at 6,200 feet with the snowcapped mountains seeming to rise out of the very banks of the cool, clean water. It's a wonder you can play here at all. Of course, some pretty good players have. Jodie Mudd won the 1980 US Golf Association Public Links championship here. And Miller Barber won a national championship when the USGA returned to Edgewood Tahoe in 1985 with the US Senior Open.

Edgewood Tahoe was built in 1968 on 250 acres originally owned by Dave and Unity Parks. The Parks had reached Tahoe by covered wagon from Missouri, bought the land, and built a home, which served as hotel and Pony Express station. Family descendants still own the land; the Parks' house, built in 1860, is still in use, too, not far from the golf course.

There's not much to Edgewood Tahoe. It's just 7,491 yards of pine trees, water, bunkers, and lovely scenery. Remember, of course, you're at 6,200 feet above sea level and ball is really going to fly,

The Lake Tahoe beach is the biggest obstacle on the 17th. And the view, of course.

so the length is not as imposing as it reads on the scorecard. The game is joined at the 488-yard, par four 2nd. The green is two tiered, and it's never any fun being on the wrong one. Next are back-to-back 602-yard par fives. Two tough par fours finish off the front nine. The 8th is 453 yards with a stream that travels up the right side and then crosses the fairway. It requires a placement drive left of the fairway pine. The 9th is 462 yards, dogleg right and tight—the toughest four par so far.

Edgewood Tahoe's final three holes are simply magnificent. The 16th is 558 yards, extremely narrow with a green heavily defended by bunkers. That's Lake Tahoe you see from the tee. The 17th plays right along the lake. It's 207 yards and fabulous, with views of trees, beach and water, bunkers, and mountains. The final hole is 574 yards and a narrow driving hole. The second shot is flanked by trees right and bunkers left. The green is guarded by water left, bunkers right and behind—not to mention the reflecting pool on your far right.

The 18th is a long, tough finishing hole along the lake with a pond guarding the left side of the green.

Glen Abbey
Ontario, Canada

How often do you get the chance to play golf where national opens are decided? In North America, anyway, the answer is "rarely." But the Canadian Open, still one of this continent's most prestigious golf tournaments, is conducted annually at the Glen Abbey Golf Club outside Toronto. The course, which incidentally is also the home of the Royal Canadian Golf Association (RCGA), is a proudly public facility. You're welcome to compare your game to such past champions as Lee Trevino, Bruce Lietzke, Greg Norman, or Curtis Strange anytime you feel up to it.

Glen Abbey was recreated by Jack Nicklaus in time for the 1977 Canadian Open. There was an original Glen Abbey on the site of the current course and somehow "rebuilt" doesn't come close to describing how much Nicklaus changed and improved the golf course. The land that Glen Abbey is built on was originally owned by a wealthy engineer who sold it to the Jesuits (hence the

The third hole is all carry over a Nicklaus-created pond to a well-bunkered green.

word "abbey" in the course's name) who, in turn, sold it to a developer. The RCGA owns it now. That original course was built entirely on a plateau that overlooks a dramatic wooded ravine carved through the centuries by Sixteen Mile Creek as it flows to Lake Ontario.

When the RCGA decided on Glen Abbey as the permanent site of their Open, Nicklaus was called upon to bring the course up to championship standards. All of the holes were redone. Greens and tees were resituated. Lakes were added and trees planted. And, most importantly, Nicklaus took advantage of the heretofore unused ravine by adding the "valley holes," which give Glen Abbey its charm and character.

The championship course is very long and very difficult. Only the supremely confident and skilled should attempt it from its full length of 7,102 yards. The greens are heavily bunkered (as are many of the landing areas) and quite contoured. After all, it was designed with the best players in the world in mind.

The back nine is Glen Abbey's beauty mark. The 11th begins the descent into the valley. The tee shot on this 452-yard par four drops over 100 feet. It's a 220 carry just to reach the fairway. Then the approach must carry Sixteen Mile Creek. Don't be embarrassed to lay up short of the water here. Plenty of great players have.

The 12th is a gorgeous and difficult par three of 187 yards over the creek to a green bunkered front and behind. The 13th is 529 with the creek crossing in front of the tee, traveling up the left side of the hole and then cut-

ting back in front of the green, perched on its stone wall, protected by a huge bunker—a beautiful hole. At the 14th you can cut off as much of the creek as prudence will allow. From the back tee, aim at the big fairway bunker and fade it. The green has a huge dip in the middle, so pick your iron carefully at this 426-yarder. The 141-yard 15th is the last hole in the valley. It's uphill, take an extra club. The 16th is 516 yards along the ravine and if you miss this heavily bunkered green left, you take the shortcut back to the valley.

The 17th and 18th holes are back on the plateau. The 434-yard 17th has 10 bunkers in the landing area and a horseshoe-shaped green with a bunker in the middle. The 18th is a great gambling hole—500 yards with water right of the green and bunkers left and behind.

Maybe you weren't playing for a national championship, but know, at least, you know what those pros who do encounter.

Down in the valley, Sixteen Mile Creek flows in front of the 12th green on its way to Lake Ontario.

47

Grand Cypress
Florida

The 9th holes of the North, left, and South nines share this huge green and the water hazard in between.

Sometimes landing safely is about all you can ask for at Grand Cypress. The grassy mounds, sand bunkers and water hazards see to that.

One shouldn't forget what a sensation Jack Nicklaus caused when people first got a look at his golf course at Grand Cypress. He took what was essentially a flat, boring Central Florida alligator farm and turned it into the talk of the town.

Today Grand Cypress' North and South (the original course) are occasionally criticized as being contrived. How soon people forget. With a few bulldozers Nicklaus made the Magic Kingdom out of milktoast. Sure, there were grassy mounds pushed up here and there, but, as dramatic as those mounds are, they're largely peripheral to the golf. What Nicklaus achieved was a unique visual presentation in a town that thrives on it.

The North's 5th is a difficult par four of 451 yards through the mounds with bunkers right of the green. The 6th plays back 561 yards, a strategic three-shot hole. The 188-yard, par three 8th is the first of two double greens. The North and South share greens on their 8th and 9th holes. The 9th is a wonderful 435-yard par four with water and waste area up the entire right side.

The South's 2nd hole sweeps right around a lake. It's a definite three-shot par five of 553 yards requir-

ing a well-placed drive and a well-placed second shot between sand and water. The third shot is across water and bunkers to a heavily protected green. Watch out for the gaggle of fairway bunkers on the left of the 570-yard 6th. Your second shot must avoid the water left and not go through the fairway into the far bunker as the hole turns left at the end. The 7th is a tough par four of 432 yards through the land of the giant mounds with fairway bunkers right and greenside bunkers left.

The 8th is quite similar to the 8th on the North. This time it's 183 yards with a deep bunker along the right, in front, and behind. The 463-yard 9th gives a considerably different look from it's counterpart on the North, though. The hole plays around the opposite side of the same lake, bending slightly left. There are no bunkers to keep you from running into the water here. The right side of the fairway features towering mounds and the green is bunkered right and behind with water front left.

And if you haven't had enough of Grand Cypress' exotica yet, there's always Nicklaus' "New Course," a dandy replica of the Old Course at St. Andrews.

Grand Traverse
Michigan

The northern coasts of Michigan's lower peninsula provide some of the most scenic land east of the Mississippi. Explored and settled by French fur traders, the area around Grand Traverse Bay includes stunning natural phenomena like Sleeping Bear Dunes National Seashore—a stretch of enormous sand dunes created by glaciers along the shore of Lake Michigan.

Literally across the street from the East Bay (Grand Traverse Bay is divided into two sections by a narrow peninsula) is the Grand Traverse Resort, a few miles outside of Traverse City. This section of northern

continued

Deep bunkers and grassy knolls guard the 17th. Lake Michigan is just over the ridge so the wind will probably be in your face.

Grand Traverse, continued

Michigan has long been known for its skiing, cherry farming, hunting and fishing. It was even the locale for Ernest Hemingway's Nick Adams stories. In the past decade or so it has become famous for its golf as well.

"The Bear" is a lovely and formidable Jack Nicklaus design created for Grand Traverse Resort and opened in 1984. Criss-crossed by creeks and dotted by marshes, farmland, and virgin woods, it is as "natural" a golf course as Nicklaus ever built. And, from the back tees this, this 7,065-yard layout certainly earns its name.

mounded green built on a peninsula with water front, right and behind. The wind off the lake will tend to push everything right. In a bit of a blow this hole is a real knee-knocker.

The 13th is another superb par three, 167 yards, downhill across a pond to a green that's framed like a Van Gogh. I don't think I'll ever tire of Nicklaus' par three holes and the assortment on this course might be the best single grouping he's ever done.

The 14th is a lovely uphill par four that plays through an old apple orchard. It's only 390 yards and sets you up for the very, very tough finish. The par five 15th plays downhill, 543 yards to a green guarded by a lake and sand bunkers. A huge tee ball that takes the roll might let you go for it in two but discretion is the better part of valor here. The 16th is a brutal uphill 451-yard par four with a deep and deadly bunker on the back right.

The 233-yard 17th is slightly downhill and the tee shot will carry an expanse of grassy mounds to a green guarded by grass and sand bunkers. The 18th is a 460-yard, dogleg right four par around a lake that protects the entire right side of the green. A perfect tee shot on the right (and risky) side of the fairway can cut 30 yards off the approach. If you can bring it home in 4-3-4 on this golf course, you've had a magnificent finish.

After a warm-up hole to open, Nicklaus challenges you with a huge, 451-yard, slightly uphill par four that plays over a deep grass bunker to a green surrounded by sand. The length here is daunting but Lake Michigan is directly at your back so the prevailing wind should be helping.

The 3rd is a relatively short par five, downhill, dogleg right. The green is reachable in two shots but presents a tiny target and is protected by a gorgeous stone-lined creek that cuts diagonally in front. The 4th is 195 yards of carry over marsh. The 168-yard 9th features a diabolically

The 451-yard 16th plays up the hill with the Northern Michigan landscape stretching out behind.

It's all humps and rolls if you get off the fairway on the 7th.

The Greenbrier
West Virginia

The Greenbrier, with its stunning trademark white Georgian portico, has been one of America's great resorts for over two hundred years. Known originally for the curative effects of its sulphur baths, it was the post-Civil War summer home of Robert E. Lee and has been a haven for generations of America's high society ever since.

The 18th is a 588-yard par five finishing hole protected by trees and deep bunkers. The gigantic green is large enough for a fiddlers' convention.

Golf came to the Greenbrier in 1910 with the creation of the original nine holes called the Lakeside—long since expanded to a full 18 holes. C.B. MacDonald built the Old White Course in 1913 and the Greenbrier course was added in 1925. The Greenbrier was revamped to a very significant degree by Jack Nicklaus in 1977 when it was designated as the site of the 1979 Ryder Cup Matches. The course was lengthened to its present 6,709 yards and par was increased from 70 to 72.

The Greenbrier sits in an upland valley of the Allegheny Mountains. The course is built on a rolling piece of ground covered with oak, pine, and maple, making autumn a particularly glorious time to play there. A pair of small lakes and a running stream form strategic hazards on seven different holes. The 2nd, 16th, and 17th, for example, play around a small lake that guards each of the

The tiny, 339-yard 10th is walled off from a creek that meanders around to front the picturesque 176-yard 11th, too.

greens on the right side.

The Greenbrier's five par three holes form a particularly interesting set of challenges. The longest is the downhill, 211-yard 7th to a green protected by a double set of bunkers on either side. The 177-yard 4th plays uphill to a mounded putting surface guarded by a huge bunker on the right front and a deep, dark ravine on the left. The 9th is just under 200 yards with one of the best bunkered greens on the golf course. The 176-yard 11th is a particularly picturesque short hole. The tee shot must carry a wide creek and a stone wall that fronts the green. That same creek forms the major hazard on the wedge-shot approach on the 339-yard 10th. The 17th is the last of the par threes, requiring a shot of 160 yards to a rela-

tively small target with a large bunker on the left and water on the right.

The dogleg left 404-yard 13th is an especially handsome four par. After driving out to the corner of the dogleg, a medium to short iron plays slightly downhill to a green framed by bunkers, trees and a scenic mountain backdrop.

The 18th is a strong and stunning finish. It's a hefty 588-yard par five to a gigantic green surrounded by bunkers. The pin placements are infinite and none of them are easy. The Greenbrier isn't a terribly long golf course, but its unusual assortment of five par threes and five par fives (two of which are under 500 yards) puts a premium on management and thoughtfulness.

Clouds drift down the Alleghany Mountain valleys behind the 406-yard 16th.

The sun sets into Calibogue Sound behind the 192-yard par three 17th green, defined by Pete Dye's railroad ties.

Harbour Town
South Carolina

Everybody has personal favorites. Maybe you had a great round there or just a great meal. Who knows? There are a million reasons. But, for me, Harbour Town Golf Links has always been a personal favorite. It's not the Spanish moss in the trees or the lighthouse or the yachts or Calibogue Sound or the marsh, though they all play a part. It's just that when I stand on the first tee I feel like I'm in a "golf" place. Everything about it seems right. And hole by hole, stroke by stroke, this Pete Dye masterpiece patiently unfolds before you. It captivates you. It's more than just a round of golf, it's a lesson. Somehow, when you're through you understand the game better than when you began.

Since 1969 Harbour Town has been the site of the PGA

The famous red and white lighthouse stands guard behind the 18th green, a splendid 478-yard par four closing hole.

Tour's Heritage Classic, won that inaugural year by Arnold Palmer. Like no other course on the PGA Tour, year in and year out the world's best seem to win at Harbour Town. Palmer. Hale Irwin. Johnny Miller. Jack Nicklaus. Hubert Green. Tom Watson. Fuzzy Zoeller. Nick Faldo. Bernhard Langer. Greg Norman. If a golf course can have no finer compliment than the list of champions who have won there, Harbour Town's history is full of high praise indeed.

At 6,912 yards it isn't overpowering by modern standards. Harbour Town's greens are very small, though, and while they're not wildly undulating

continued

A pesky pine guards the approach to the dogleg left 16th. Placement of the drive is always a key at Harbour Town.

they are subtly contoured. The tee shot is absolutely crucial. You simply must place the ball in the proper spot in the fairway. Miss and you can take the bogey to the bank.

The 9th and the 13th holes, tiny par fours of 337 yards and 378 yards, are illustrative of the point. The 9th has tall pines that block any tee shot played too far to the left. If, however, you find the rough by sliding too far right, you won't be able to stop the ball on this shallow green. Behind it is a pot bunker that has instantaneous double-

bogey written all over it. The 13th is similar. There is a very narrow neck of fairway that must be found. If you wind up under the oaks left or right the only option is to punch it forward into the huge collar bunker that surrounds the front and sides of the green and hope you don't end up unplayable against the railroad ties.

Harbour Town's finish is as fine as any in the world. The 575-yard, par five 15th is a true three-shot hole. No one with any sense ever thinks about going for this tiny green in two. The hole is very narrow and it doglegs left the last few yards around a pond. A perfect layup leaves a full wedge into a target that looks about the size of a dime. The 16th, at 376 yards, is another one of those short par fours that requires a perfect tee shot to avoid the pine tree in the right part of the fairway and the waste bunker on the left. The 17th is one of the prettiest par threes anywhere. This 192-yarder can play anywhere from a 6-iron to a 1-iron, depending on the wind off Calibogue Sound. As for the 18th, who hasn't seen that red-and-white lighthouse looming in the distance on this 478-yard monster? The tee shot takes a big carry over marsh to a generous landing area. Then it takes an even better second to carry the marsh and the bunker to get home. A great hole to cap off a great experience.

The narrow 9th hole is short and dangerous with deep bunkers in front and behind.

Heather Glen

South Carolina

The 18th is a terrific par five that turns right at the end, playing over water to a crowned green.

Bulkheading and pot bunkers add a touch of Scotland to Heather Glen.

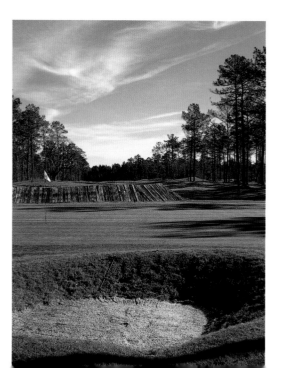

For the record, the reason Heather Glen Golf Links is included in this book is not because of the Scottish leitmotif the course has embraced. In fact, it's included in spite of it. Personally, I've never been one who believed in the "wee bit of Scotland" concept of golf course architecture.

The reason Heather Glen is featured here is that, regardless of the hype, this is a truly fine, truly American golf course. What Willard Byrd built here on the border between North and South Carolina is no imitation, it's a great golf course in its own right.

The 4th, for instance, is 180 yards over sand, love grass, and Scotch broom. There's a bunker behind the green, too. The 6th is a devil. A sand bunker with a tree at the entrance and a couple more at the exit runs for 150 or so yards up the right side. If you keep your drive to the left (which you must), you can get home but it's a tough spot to hit. The 9th is a monster 447-yard dogleg left with fairway bunkers

left and right and a creek left and short of the landing area to catch your snap hooks. Your second may be blind but there's a pine tree behind the green with a white dot to give you a line. Beware the big bunker on the left. This baby is uphill, into the wind and just plain hard, making it the toughest hole on the golf course.

On the back the 13th is another diabolical par three. It's 165 yards with lots of mounds. There's one bunker called "Devil's Mistress"— you don't want to find out why.

The 14th has the creek running along the left and a gaggle of bunkers short of the green. The par five 15th doglegs right with the creek running on the left before crossing in front of the bowl-shaped green.

The final three holes are simply magnificent. The 16th is close to perfect. It's 375 yards, dogleg left, creek, bunkers, waste area a tough green, mounded and guarded by one pot bunker. The 17th has two routes, safe and daring. Go for it— a simply exquisite 409-yard hole. The 587-yard 18th is a superb finisher, reachable in two because of the sharp right turn at the end, but it's risky.

Heritage
South Carolina

The Heritage Club is perched overlooking an expanse of marsh and the Intracoastal Waterway.

The Heritage Club was the collaborative effort of developer Larry Young and architect Dan Maples. After previous successes at Marsh Harbour and Oyster Bay, the Heritage Club near Pawley's Island has rapidly come to be regarded as one of the finest golf courses along South Carolina's Grand Strand.

Built on the former location of the True Blue and Midway plantations, the Heritage Club stretches to a demanding 7,100 yards and plays to a par of 71. Southern history and hospitality seem to drip from its Spanish moss-laden oaks. An old, forgotten cemetery flanks the 4th green, one of the prettiest and most difficult holes on the course. Boats sailing on the Waccamaw River can be seen cruising slowly by in the distance. The tee shot on this 440-yarder has to be perfectly

The 570-yard 2nd hole is an ingenious par five with a second-shot landing area on each side of the water.

placed to avoid a large oak on the right side of the fairway. Anything too far left, though, and the approach to the green is blocked out by more trees.

Another truly outstanding golf hole is the 570-yard 2nd. After a drive that avoids a pair of large bunkers on the right, the second shot calls for a decision on whether to play across a sliver of water that bisects the fairway or stay to the right of it. The safer play is to the right but be certain to take enough club to clear the clump of trees that could block your approach to the green. Don't even think about getting home in two. Coming into this well-bunkered green with a short iron from either side of the water is no picnic.

The 2nd through the sixth holes is a very tough stretch of the golf course, but it's not the toughest you're going to encounter. Lucky 13 is a mere 235-yard par three, and

most of that yardage represents carry over water. The green is huge, but it's a frightening shot no matter how you look at it.

The 14th turns the screw a little tighter with a 440-yard par four, dogleg left. The tee shot is across water and you have to know where to aim and how much to cut off. And then you have to do it. The second shot is also across water, usually a mid to long iron to a severely sloped green.

Straightaway, the 460-yard, par four 15th is just long, longer, longest. The 17th is a terrific hole. It's a 440-yard, dogleg right, but it's the Scottish "look" of the pot bunkers fronting the green that gives this hole its special feel.

The final hole is a good chance to get back one of those shots you dropped along the way. Nothing like finishing with a birdie. The tee shot is the crucial play on this 530-yard, dogleg left par five. Once you're around the corner, the green is reachable but dangerously so—there's water in front, mounds and bunkers behind. An easy layup to full wedge distance will give you a good chance for that strong finish.

The 13th, in the foreground, is a long, hard par three. Across a neck of water the 18th doglegs left and plays to a green heavily protected by water and mounds.

The Homestead
Virginia

The elegant red brick Homestead, tucked majestically away in Virginia's Allegheny Mountains, has been entertaining guests from Washington and Jefferson all the way to weekend hackers since before America was born. The Hot Springs resort was founded in 1766, growing up around the warm waters so prized by previous generations for their therapeutic effect.

The first golf course, the Homestead, was built in 1892. In 1923 William Flynn created the famous Upper Cascades, a course that has been held in the highest esteem ever since. The Upper Cascades is the course where Sam Snead caddied as a youngster and learned the game of golf. And no trip to Hot Springs would be complete without a meal at Sam Snead's Tavern, the centerpiece of the tiny town. In fact, don't be too surprised if you see Sam himself. He still lives nearby, as does his nephew, J.C., who plays out of the Homestead.

The Upper Cascades is a rolling mountain course of 6,566 yards, par 71, located just a few miles south of Hot Springs. It's a tight course that plays longer than the yardage would indicate because so many of the holes seem to be uphill. And watch out for the pines. These trees are not like the tall pines of North Carolina or Georgia. These evergreens have limbs that go all the way to the ground. Roll you ball under

The Homestead's stately red brick hotel sits just beyond the 18th hole of the original Homestead course.

ravine of about 140 yards. A big hit will reach a second plateau in the fairway leaving 170 to 190 to the green. But if you hang up in between levels it's a tough shot off the slope.

The 12th is a short five par from the back tees or a killer four par from the whites. Either way, with hazard left and mountains right, it's as tight as any hole on the golf course. The 15th is a big three par of 222 yards out of a tight chute. The 16th and 17th holes are a pair of interesting back-to-back par fives. A stream runs the entire length of the 16th on the right,

The Cascades Course was carved out of the rolling Alleghany Mountain woods in 1924.

one of them and it gives a whole new meaning to the concept of "jail." You're lucky if you can punch an iron back into play.

The 4th is the first of a fine set of par three holes. It's just under 200 yards from an elevated tee to a green that sits on a sidehill. Anything left rolls down into a bunker and under the dreaded evergreens and anything right is dead, too. The 5th is an unreachable par five of 576 yards with a hazard on the left. The 9th is a superb 450-yard four par. The drive is from an elevated tee and must carry a

dumping into a pond in front of the green. It's possible to go for the green in two shots but anything over winds up dead under the evergreens. The smarter play is a layup with a mid-iron. The 17th is a short par five of just 485 yards with mountainside left and underbrush (and a lost ball) right. A couple of small ponds protect the green and if you lose it right you find the hazard. The Upper closes with another fine three par, the 192-yard 18th guarded by a lake in front and bunkers left and right. Actually, maybe now would be the best time for Sam Snead's Tavern.

Hominy Hill
New Jersey

The clubhouse at Hominy Hill, site of the '83 U.S. Public Links Championship, is a converted dairy barn.

Hominy Hill is hearty stock from humble beginnings. Originally a dairy farm, Henry Mercer commissioned Robert Trent Jones to build a golf course there in 1964. The clubhouse is, in fact, a converted dairy barn. The Monmouth County Park System purchased Hominy Hill Golf Course from the Mercer family in 1977, thereby creating one of the finest public golf courses in America.

From the back tees Hominy Hill stretches out to 7,059 very difficult yards. Relatively flat, it's heavily bunkered and makes strategic use of a stream and a pond. In the 1983 US Public Links Championship held there the lowest score was a 69.

The stream first comes into play as it runs behind the green on the 542-yard, par five 4th. On the 207-yard 11th the tee shot must carry the stream which then runs up the left side of the green. And on the 535-yard 14th the water runs in front of the green making any attempt to get home in two shots a perilous adventure at best. Ditto for the 9th hole, a double dogleg of 513 yards, that plays toward and then around a pond.

While the water hazards are cleverly used, the course is truly characterized more by its 100-plus sand bunkers. For example, the 537-yard, dead-straight 17th has a huge fairway bunker on the right in the first landing area, then bunkers left and right in the second landing zone and a bunkered green. The 18th is a dogleg right with the road on the right and bunkers left off the tee. The green is also well bunkered.

It's what became known as typical Robert Trent Jones—long and difficult.

The 16th is a long par three of 209 yards but you don't want to go over this green.

Horseshoe Bay
Texas

About an hour's drive west of Austin in the Texas Hill Country hard by Lake LBJ is the largest Robert Trent Jones Sr. laboratory in the world. Jones built his first course at Horseshoe Bay, Slick Rock, in 1974. In 1979 he added the longer and more difficult Ram Rock. And then in 1986 Jones tacked on the stunning Applerock just for good measure. No other resort in the United States boasts three RTJ Sr. golf courses, and so enticing are they as a group that it's just about impossible to choose between them.

The 18th is elevated and well guarded. It's not wise to be above the hole.

The granddaddy, Slick Rock, recently spent about a million dollars to put in a waterfall on the 14th hole just to spruce things up a bit. The rolling Applerock has the most commanding views of the magnificent scenery. Shot for shot, though, Ram Rock probably edges them out at the tape.

Ram Rock's 2nd hole is a huge sweeping dogleg right with trees and a bunker protecting the corner. It takes a big drive just to be able to see the green for your second shot. The 3rd hole is another big par four playing 442. The green is protected in the front by bunkers left and right.

The closing hole on the front is not likely to be soon forgotten. The 9th is a 540-yard, par five dogleg left that narrows down with water left and right of the green and stretching down both sides of the fairway for the final 150 yards.

There are a few more Texas-size holes on the back, too. The 13th sweeps left and plays 438 yards. There are large bunkers left and behind the green. The 14th is a real three-shot par five. It measures 541 yards and bends hard right. Off the tee you must thread the needle between trees left and right and avoid the fairway bunker on the left. You're second must come up short of three cross bunkers in front of Trent's Burn.

The 16th is a gorgeous golf hole. It's a 417-yard dogleg right with water right of the green and sand and trees left. It's a very narrow opening and requires a superb second shot. The 17th is a lot of carry uphill on this 214-yard par three.

Ram Rock's challenging 14th hole runs 541 yards downhill to a green protected by sand and water. The third shot here can be from a testy sidehill, downhill lie.

Innisbrook
Florida

A lay up short of the water on the right is the best play on this short par four, the third hole on Copperhead #2—the 12th on the championship layout.

The tall pines. The cypress trees moored in the ponds. The Spanish Moss draped from limbs like a fine filigree. Add just about perfect weather, an egret or two, and a superb golf course designed by E.L. Packard and what you have is Innisbrook, a little slice of heaven on a thousand acres in a pine forest north of Tampa.

The golf course, naturally, is the renowned Copperhead—the 1st and 2nd nines of the current 27 holes that bares that name. It would be remiss not to mention the other two fine Innisbrook courses, Sandpiper and Island. The latter was the site of the 1990 NCAA Championship and has a stretch of holes—the 6th, 7th, and 8th—that is about as demanding a loop as you'll find.

At any rate, it's the bite of the Copperhead that you're likely to remember best. Packard finished the 7,031-yard, par 71 course in 1972 and from the very first shot it has been considered among Florida's finest. In 1990 it became the site of the J.C. Penney Mixed Team Championship, held for years a few miles farther south in Bardmoor.

The opening hole is a 540-yard par five that breaks right at the end around a lake. The tee shot is downhill, and you can cut that little corner at the end to get home in two. You have to go over the lake and over a huge bunker to do it, though. If you decide to lay-up in the neck of the fairway, too much club will find a bunker there.

The 4th is a beauty of a short par three, just 165 yards with bunkers and pine trees everywhere. The 5th is a 539-yard par five, uphill. The landing area is protected by bunkers on either side. The hole turns left at the end and frequently just blasting away with a 3-wood second leaves you

Copperhead's No. 4 hole is surrounded by pine trees dripping Spanish Moss and Innisbrook's ever-present sand.

nothing better than a long bunker shot for your third. The 6th is a man-size par four of 459 back down the hill. It swings slightly right and the lake is not really in play but the second shot is extremely difficult.

The 10th (or 1st hole on Copperhead's number two nine) is only 451 and straightaway. Huff. Puff. The 11th is a long, straight 552-yard five par to a very heavily bunkered green. The 14th is another of the double-dogleg par fives. This one is 571 and a great hole. There's water in the landing area for the second shot so stay to the left.

The 16th will really get your attention: dogleg right, water on the right, and a mere 465 yards, par four. The 17th is 211 yards to a green bunkered on both sides and behind. The 18th plays 424 uphill with fairway bunkers on the left and greenside bunkers front left and back right. It can be a brutal finish.

The 18th of the championship layout (No. 9 on Copperhead #2) is uphill and heavily bunkered all the way.

The prairie grasses make good grazing for the elk but trouble for wayward shots to the seventh hole.

Jackson Hole Golf & Tennis Club stretches out in the valley below the magnificent Grand Tetons.

Jackson Hole
Wyoming

Everyone should see the Grand Tetons in the golden early morning light. Dawn in Jackson Hole is pure magic. In that setting golf takes on a mystical quality. To be able to play this aggravating little game in the crisp air alongside the Teton's sharp-edged peaks swathed in sweet colors is an experience you'll not soon forget.

Jackson Hole Golf and Tennis Club makes it all the more magical by the quality of the course. Originally designed by Bob Baldock in 1963, the course lies eight miles north of Jackson at the edge of the Teton National Park in a flat valley at the base of the mountains. Its holes are strung out in the woods, prairie grass, and wildflowers along the Gros Ventre river and a series of creeks that feed into it. In 1967 Robert Trent Jones Jr.

reworked fifteen of the eighteen greens and replaced and resituated all the tees, creating what is today a 7,168-yard masterpiece. It was the site of the 1988 US Public Links Championship and will host the 1993 Women's US Public Links.

Bring your driver when you play Jackson Hole. In fact, bring two—you might just wear the first one out. At 6,209 feet above sea level, there's about a ten percent boost in distance, making the 7,000-plus yards a less disheartening. And Jackson Hole is a fairly open golf course. You're pretty much allowed to let it fly off the tee.

On the 351-yard, slightly downhill 1st hole, you just might drive the green. Don't start thinking that this golf course is going to be a pushover, though. The 581-yard 2nd is a

continued

The pond in front of the 169-yard 13th is a perfect reflecting pool for the Grand Tetons. Also a collector of golf balls.

The dogleg left 394-yard 5th hole is bunkered on all sides at the green.

strong three-shot par five. With a feeder creek all along the right side and then crossing in front of the green, creating ponds left and right, it's a smart play to try and make birdie with your wedge. The 8th is another strong par five of nearly 600 yards with the river fronting the green once again. The Gros Ventre is all along the left on the 439-yard 9th.

The 169-yard 13th is simply stunning. The pond in the front of the green is a reflecting pool for the Grand Tetons. The 438-yard 14th has a creek on the right while the 15th is straight and 449. The green of the 203-yard 16th is probably the best-bunkered on the course. The 17th is a 412-yard dog-leg left, and you finish with a 552-yard dogleg right that features a series of bunkers and water short and right of the green. Regardless of your score, you're likely to never have a more satisfying day on a golf course.

Jasper Park

Alberta, Canada

Obviously you don't want to fly it over the elevated third green, a very difficult 454-yard dogleg right par four.

The 4th is a 240-yard par three, usually into the wind. The bunkers catch anything that strays.

Jasper Park is another magnificent mountain masterpiece by Stanley Thompson. Built in 1925 in Jasper National Park a little over 170 miles north of Banff, the course nestles up to Lac Beauvert in the midst of the Maligne Mountains in the Canadian Rockies. Uniquely, a majority of the holes have been designed to play directly at distant (or not-so-distant) peaks.

At approximately 3,500 feet above sea level, the 6,598-yard, par 71 course certainly isn't overpowering-ly long. You'll find, however, that clubbing yourself correctly will be something of a challenge. Part of the deception is caused by the vastness of the mountains and part by the altitude. In addition, Thompson's bunkering will occasionally create a trompe l'oeil, making it difficult for you to convince yourself to hit enough club.

After a benign beginning, the 454-yard, par four dogleg right 3rd presents a very stiff challenge. It's 265 yards over the trees on the right to the corner. The green is small and elevated with bunkers on all sides. The 4th is a 240-yard par three over a brace of bunkers. The right greenside bunker is particularly dangerous because the green slopes away.

Don't go left on the 7th. The 178-yard par three plays over a creek, and anything that hits left runs down into heavy woods. The trick on the 417-yard 8th is to find a level lie for your second shot. It's a hard green to hit from a sidehill, downhill stance.

The drive on the 483-yard, par five 10th should be toward the pinwheel fairway bunker on the right. Though the green is surrounded with sand, you can get home in two. The 13th hole is a true three-shotter, however. It's 603 yards of rolling fairway that narrows down to a hidden green. The edge of Lac Beauvert is the setting for the gorgeous 361-yard 14th.

The 15th is called "Bad Baby." It's just 138 yards long but drops off in every direction. The 369-yard 16th also has the lake on the left and in front of the green, making it a very tight driving hole. The 360-yard 17th provides a much more receptive target. The green is heavily bunkered but a wedge or short iron here should give you a run at birdie. The closing hole is probably the toughest on the golf course. It's a 463-yard, dogleg left par four with bunkers surrounding the green.

Since 1926 Jasper Park has staged a tournament called the Totem Pole. Bing Crosby won it in 1947. If Jasper Park was good enough for Bing, it's good enough for me.

Jasper Park is nestled in the fir trees in the midst of the majestic Canadian Rockies.

Kananaskis
Alberta, Canada

The Kananaskis River winds throughout the Mt. Lorette Course brushing up against the 14th green here.

It seems as though the river and the mountains are always in play at Kananaskis.

When the province of Alberta decided to build a championship golf facility, it just made sense that Robert Trent Jones would be the architect. With Banff Springs and Jasper Park—the two world-famous courses by Jones' mentor, Stanley Thompson—so close by, it seemed a natural fit.

Jones almost simultaneously built two strong, eighteen-hole courses at Kananaskis. The first, Mount Lorette (named for the peak that dominates the course), was completed in 1983. It was followed a year later by the Mount Kidd course. Both are excellent layouts, though

Mount Lorette is probably the favored of the two, in a photo finish—which can be quite stunning when you're around 5,000 feet above sea level in the Canadian Rockies.

The Kananaskis River twists and turns throughout, and it or its feeder creeks come into play on eight of Mount Lorette's holes. And if the wind is up, it can swirl in the mountain valleys in unpredictable ways making club selection a gruesome undertaking.

The opening hole provides a very tough beginning. It's a 412-yard par four with water on the left and a creek along the right, encouraging something less than a driver. The creek continues up the right hand side along the large but well-bunkered green.

Another highlight is the 4th hole, a beautiful but extremely long par three, playing 254 yards from the back tee—most of the time into the wind. The 7th is another par four as big as all outdoors, measuring 482 yards. The driving area is quite large, though there is a bunker in the middle of the fairway that will catch any drive that isn't hit on the screws. The green is generous in size to accommodate the long second shot but, again, heavily bunkered.

Mount Lorette's 14th hole is a lovely five par of 523 yards that begins with a fairly broad landing area but narrows down with the Kananaskis River on the right and bunkers on the left at the green—a bit too risky to try to reach in two.

The finishing hole is another big par four of 463 yards. It plays to a slick, kidney-shaped double green (the 9th of the Mount Kidd course is on the other side) with bunkers front, back, and to the side and a creek cutting across in front.

Kemper Lakes

Illinois

With water left and right and bunkers all around, the 18th green is tough to hit if you're not in the fairway.

The approach to 8th green must guard against going left into the water but, when the pin is down in front, missing it right in the bunker leaves a nasty little shot, too.

When it comes to Kemper Lakes Golf Course, the accent's on the "lake." Built on marsh and farmland in Lake County, Illinois, in 1979 by the Kemper Group, Kemper Lakes Golf Course is one of the "youngest" courses ever to host a major championship—the 1989 PGA, won by Payne Stewart in his Chicago Bear knickers. It's also one of the few daily-fee courses to be so honored. It was designed by Ken Killian and Dick Nugent.

Kemper Lakes can be stretched to 7,217 yards from the back tees, though in the PGA Championship it was played slightly less, a paltry 7,197. And, believe me, the players were grateful for those 20 yards. Kemper Lakes plays very long.

For instance, the 5th is a 442-yard par four, o.b. left with a stand of nettlesome pines on the right. The 7th is a tough par five of 557 yards. There are bunkers on both sides in the landing area, and any hooked shot will find the lake on the left. The second shot must land safely between two fairway bunkers right and the water left. Avoid the greenside bunker left with your pitch shot, as it runs down into the water. The 8th is a 421-yard, dogleg left where you must thread your drive down the middle. If you go too far, however, the pines on the right come into play where the hole bends. The green is guarded by water left and a large bunker right. You finish off the front with a big, uphill 448-yard four par. There are large bunkers both in the fairway and around the green.

The major peril on the 453-yard 10th is the fairway bunker on the right. If you hit the Big Sky Hook it's possible to find water left. The 11th is a 534-yard, par five, and a well-struck drive can catch the downslope and give you a reasonable shot at reaching the green in two.

The 13th is 219 with three large bunkers and three tiers on the green. The 14th hole is a dogleg left par four of 420 yards. A huge fairway bunker

guards the left. The green is small, double tiered, and well bunkered. The 15th is an enormous par five of 578 yards. There's no getting home here. Bunkers in the landing area. Another bunker and trees in the valley on the layup shot. A tough little pitch. Five is a good score. The 16th is the meanest hole on the golf course. It's 469 yards with water on the right, fairway bunkers left and water in front and right of the green.

The 17th is 203 yards across the lake. The 18th has some fascinating history. During an exhibition when the tees were up on this 433-yard sharp dogleg left, Greg Norman took his driver and went across the lake straight at the green, reaching the greenside bunker. Don't even think about it.

The 10th is one of Kemper Lakes' many giant par fours. It measures 453 yards to a bunkered green.

Kiawah
South Carolina

When the Landmark Land Company was given the opportunity to host the 1991 Ryder Cup on Kiawah Island, it commissioned Pete Dye to design the course to host this prestigious international event. The land where the golf course was to be plotted is probably the last piece of ocean-front property on the eastern seaboard that will ever be devoted exclusively to golf. It's a skinny spit of land made up of sand dunes and marsh, probably not suitable for commercial development but wonderfully fit for golf.

Dye met the challenge with the large-scale Ocean Course. If played at the very back tees, it could reach 7,786 yards. Of course, no one in their right mind has any intention of playing it from back there. The notion was to allow teeing options depending on the wind. For the Ryder Cup the tees were set something in the 7,240 range, still titanic.

With the exception of a few marsh holes, the golf course is basically treeless. It plays down and back between rows of natural beach dunes. Seldom are you more than one fairway removed from the sea. The first four holes play in an easterly direction with the ocean on the right; the next nine holes play to the west with the ocean on the left; and the final five holes play back east with the Atlantic on the right again. The second tee is the farthest point from the ocean and you drive the ball directly at the sea. The fairways are quite wide and most of the

The 7th hole is the shortest par five but can stretch to 569 yards. That's the Atlantic Ocean in the near background.

Pete Dye's 478-yard 18th requires two wood shots, especially if played into the wind. A score of par 4 is nothing to frown about here.

greens are surrounded with closely mown dwarf grass allowing low, running shots underneath the wind and generous use of the "Texas wedge" for those balls that trickle off the edges and run down embankments or into deep swales.

The 4th and 9th holes on the front will give you an idea of the dimensions of this course. The 4th is a 465-yard—these are tournament yardages, now, not all the way back—par four that requires a tee shot of around 230 in the air over marsh just to reach the fairway. The long second shot must also carry marsh. The 9th hole is 462 yards, dogleg left. About 50 yards short of the green a sand dune juts into the fairway. The green has a bunker left that's eight or 10 feet below the putting surface and a pot bunker halfway up the green on the right.

The three finishing holes are extraordinarily difficult. The par five 16th plays 605 yards. The tee shot must carry water and sand with a lake on the left of the two-tiered fairway. The landing area is literally just yards away from the ocean. The fairway curves back left and there's a wastebunker between the second landing area and the ocean. The third shot is uphill to a green set back in the dunes. The 17th plays 194 yards to a shallow green, over a lake and cattails. The 18th is the last of the big par fours—470 yards with a roller coaster fairway, going up, bending right, and heading down into a swale and the green, protected by sand in front, dunes, and sea oats.

Kingsmill
Virginia

Kingsmill's River Course, designed by Pete Dye, is the host of the PGA Tour's Anheuser-Busch Classic. It may also be one of the most historic courses in the United States—not because it's the home of Curtis Strange, winner of the 1988 and 1989 US Opens (though it is), but because, during the building of the course a number of Native American and Colonial archeological sites were discovered, yielding a wealth of fascinating artifacts. The golf course is dotted with plantation house ruins, a tribal village site, and Colonial artillery emplacements that defended the James River. Kingsmill's Conference Center is built on the site of Burwell's Landing, one of the major docking facilities serving Colonial Williamsburg.

What with Yorktown a few miles to the east and Williamsburg a couple of miles to the northwest, Kingsmill is a heavenly retreat for the historically minded. And if you're not much into history, Busch Gardens is right there to provide a thrill or two.

The golf course will give you a couple of thrills all its own. It's 6,776 yards and, like most Dye courses, puts more of a premium on thought and position than sheer power.

The 4th is the first of three very demanding four pars on the front side. It's 437 yards with a fairway that doglegs slightly left and cants slightly right to left toward a creek running down in the woods. The 5th is a pretty par three that plays across that creek. The 8th and 9th holes are two tough back-to-back fours. The 8th requires a perfect tee shot, usually with a 1-iron or 3-wood, that has to be far enough left to give you a clear shot at the green but not so far left that it trickles into Wareham's Pond. The 9th is a 452-yard, dead-ahead four par to an elevated green protected by bunkers on the right.

The 10th is the third challenging par four in a row. It

plays 431 yards with bunkers guarding the left side of the fairway and virtually the entire green. The 11th through the very, very narrow 15th (don't lose your approach to the right here) will give you a few chances at birdie. Considering the three finishing holes ahead, it would be a good idea to make a couple of them.

The 16th is a 427-yard par four. The drive has to be long enough to reach the corner on this dogleg right. The second, usually a mid-iron, is played to probably the best protected green on the golf course. There are deep bunkers and tough sidehill lies to catch any approach that misses this multitiered green.

The 17th is a lovely 177-yarder right along the river. Anything right is dead, deader, deadest. The 18th is a tough 438-yard four par. The hole has been changed since the course opened, with the original green serving as the 18th on the newer Plantation Course. The new hole is more straightaway with the tee shot over a lake to an undulating fairway. The second plays slightly uphill to a newly constructed, well-contoured, and well-bunkered green.

The 2nd hole on Pete Dye's River Course is a 204-yard par three with an undulating green and deep bunkers.

The James River and Kingsmill's par three course are in the distance looking back from the new 18th green.

La Costa
California

The inclusion of the La Costa Resort & Spa is not entirely above board. The course dealt with here—the one both the regular and senior PGA Tours play in the season-opening Tournament of Champions—isn't a golf course at all. The "championship" layout is formed by taking nine holes from La Costa's North Course and nine from the South.

The mere mortal can't play them in that order. In effect, to play the "championship" course you either have to go 36 holes in one day or stay an extra night at this luxurious resort and play two days in a row—tough break.

For a few years La Costa was better known for mud baths and massage than for golf. The conditioning of the two Dick Wilson layouts had deteriorated somewhat but an infusion of cash from new owner Sport Shinko in 1987 restored golf to its position of prominence.

The front nine of the tournament course is comprised of North 1, 2, 3, 4, 14, 15, 16, 17 and 18. The toughest among them is the championship 5th (North No. 14). It's 446 with a creek running up the left side and then crossing the fairway about 300 to 320 yards out. The green is small and bunkered front and back. A very difficult four.

The championship 7th (North No. 16) is a picturesque three par of 188 yards full carry over water. The 9th (North No. 18) is a thoughtful 538-yard par five. Frequently into the wind, the majority of the time the second shot will be a layup short of the creek that crosses the fairway. But, if you bust a drive and avoid the fairway bunkers and the wind is not too severe, you might give it a go in two.

The tournament back nine corresponds to the South Course back nine. The 10th is a huge, straight-away four par of 450 yards. There are huge bunkers left and trees right making for a tiny landing area. The second shot must carry a lake to another well-bunkered green. Four is an excellent score here.

The final four holes of LaCosta's South— and, thus, tourna-ment—Course turn directly into the pre-vailing ocean wind. The 15th is 378, dogleg left. From the elevated tee all you see are trees and a creek—miss them. Place your tee shot on the right side if you want to see the pin.

The 16th is a 432-yard par four that plays long, longer, longest. Pine trees pre-sent a thorny problem on the right side of the dogleg, so keep it honest here. The 17th is a 569-yarder with a lake guarding the right side of the hole from about 250 yards all the way to the green. Keep your second shot well left. The finishing hole is 421 yards, par four, dogleg right. The left fairway bunker is oblivion. Three large bunkers sur-round the green.

Now it's time for that massage.

The 421 yard 18th on the South (and Tournament 18th) usually plays into the wind. A lot of strokes have been lost in that leftside fairway bunker.

Las Hadas
Mexico

The port city of Manzanillo, tucked away in one of the bays where the Sierra Madre mountains meet the Pacific, has served as safe haven for sailors from Sir Francis Drake to Cortez. Just across the bay from the city, out at the end of Santiago Peninsula, the white Moorish spires of Las Hadas push up into the azure sky.

Roy Dye designed this 6,495-yard tester called La Mantarraya. Length is not a factor here but there is trouble everywhere. The idea is to pick your spots, scurry around a bit, and survive.

The strongest hole on the opening nine is the 3rd, a 570 yard par five requiring a daring tee shot across a water hazard and a second shot short of a huge bunker in the middle of the fairway. The 4th is just 383 yards, but there's sand all the way up the right side. The 7th is 375 with a double fairway and danger in between.

Water can come into play if you stray too far left on the tiny 313-yard 10th. The green is completely surrounded with sand. The 11th is 498 and reachable but it takes a very precise drive in a narrow area right or left and then a bold second shot over bunkers. The 12th is 409, again with two possible landing areas. The green is guarded by a stretch of sand in front. The 15th is a terrific 524-yard par five that calls for a drive across water. Once in the fairway, it's possible to cut the dogleg and go for the green in two but you have to cross a wasteland to get there.

The finish at Las Hadas is right along the bay. The 17th is the best hole on the golf course. It's 432 yards, across water to a patch of fairway in the middle of the beach. The second shot is across water to an isolated green protected by sand. The 18th, which is being redesigned, plays 160 yards across the Pacific to a green set on a point out in the sea.

Mauna Kea
Hawaii

Forget all those cute little "paradise" lines that open almost any golf story about the Hawaiian Islands. Mauna Kea is beyond paradise. Because of the ocean waves pounding the coast? The snow-capped Mauna Kea volcano? The black lava beds? The whales that winter off the Kohala Coast? The plus-perfect weather?

All of the above. And the fact that Robert Trent Jones may have done his very finest work right here. Certainly, it's some of the most beautiful work anyone has ever done in the game of golf.

Consider that before Jones struck a pact with Laurance Rockefeller in 1962, nothing outside of a few scattered cactus plants was able to grow on the five-thousand-year-old lava beds in the shadow of Mauna Kea. Jones crushed lava

rocks and combined that with another layer of crushed coral to form the soil base. Water was provided by a well. The solution seems simple enough today. But in 1964 when Arnold Palmer, Gary Player, and Jack Nicklaus officially opened the course with an exhibition round, the green fairways of Mauna Kea strung out on the black lava seemed like a miracle.

This golf course might be set in paradise, but it also happens to be one of the world's toughest tests of the golf. In fact, a few thought it too tough in its original form. So, in 1975 Jones' son, Robert Trent Jones Jr., was commissioned to reconstruct and ease seven

continued

One-shot holes don't get much harder than the 11th. It plays 247 yards downhill toward the Pacific.

It should be quite plain why Mauna Kea's third hole is considered one of the most beautiful in the world.

Everything kicks left around the 14th green but a miss to the right could spell disaster.

The par five 10th can be reached with two very good shots but the percentage play is a lay-up second and a ittle pitch for your third.

Mauna Kea, continued.

greens. A few modifications have been made since but the basic course remains the work of Jones & Son.

Very little of Mauna Kea actually abuts the ocean—mostly the course follows the contours of the lava flows across the uniquely undulating terrain. But it is definitely a seaside course. Playing from the very back, or black tees, Mauna Kea is a daunting challenge on a calm day. Any kind of sustained, brisk ocean breeze can make the 7,114-yard "blacks" virtually impossible. For that reason, a wide variety of teeing positions (up to six on some holes) are available. Unlike most courses where there is a big dropoff from the championship to the regular tees, Mauna Kea has a set of blue tees that measure 6,737 yards. I strongly suggest considering them. In this case pride goeth before the double-bogey.

Jones immediately stuns you on the 3rd—one of the most beautiful holes in golf. It's been compared frequently to Cypress Point's 16th. The shocking thing is that it's a good comparison, though Mauna Kea's contribution isn't quite as hard as Cypress'. The 3rd hole at Mauna Kea plays 210 yards across a Pacific Ocean inlet. The green has a string of bunkers in front, a couple behind and one right. But, from 210 yards, those bunkers look more like catchers' mitts and safe haven. Four is a good score here, but simply having played it is good enough.

There is another three par that gets noticed a little bit. It'll get your attention, for sure. The 11th is a 247-yard one-shotter to a green bunkered left, right and behind. It plays shorter because the tee is elevated almost 100 feet. Of course, it also plays directly toward the ocean and, thus, into whatever wind is blowing. Some days it's the shortest par four on the course.

Interestingly, the four finishing holes are the same from the black or the blue tees. The 15th is a 201-yard three par

to a green narrow and bunkered in the front (the toughest pin) and wide in the back. The 16th is a big 422-yarder, slight dogleg right to a well-guarded green. The 17th is 555 yards, dogleg left, long and tough. The closing hole is 428 yards with the tee a couple of hundred feet above the fairway.

The elevated green on the 409-yard 13th presents a very small target.

Mauna Lani
Hawaii

About the worst thing you can say about the Francis H. I'i Brown Course at Mauna Lani is that it doesn't exist anymore. Actually, that's not quite accurate. It has simply divided and multiplied. The original course set in the black lava flows at Kalahuipua on the Kohala Coast of the Big Island has been split in half. Two new nines have been created, and now this Hawaiian jewel built in 1981 will comprise one half of the North Course and one half of the South.

For some reason, golf courses over time seem to resist this kind of convenient dividing and remixing. It's as if the integrity of the original design demands that it eventually be restored. The North and South courses at Mauna Lani may be the exception. Certainly the new holes seem to give every indication of being the equal of the old. But, for old times sake, we'll deal here with the world renowned original—the Francis H. I'i Brown Course.

The names most closely associated with the design and construction of Mauna Lani's first golf course are Raymond Cain and Homer Flint. From its opening this stunning layout captured the world's imagination set as it was against the crashing surf and stark black lava, punctuated with palms, kiawa trees, and rolling green fairways. Incredibly photogenic, it remains one of the most strikingly beautiful golf courses ever built.

The front nine plays over a rough form of lava called "a'a." The opening hole is a dogleg right par five of 535 yards with a tee shot that plays along King's Trail, a historic pre-

serve and a route that once encircled the entire island. There's plenty of room right as the first and ninth fairways adjoin. The green is protected in front by three bunkers. The 3rd hole is the first of Mauna Lani's spectacular par threes. It plays 202 yards over a lake toward the ocean. The 4th is a breathtaking short par four of 387 yards dogleg right. The drive is directly toward the ocean to a landing area bunkered on both sides. The hole turns to parallel the rocks and pounding surf. The green is guarded by a bunker right and the Pacific left.

The 5th hole plays downhill 413 yards, bending sharply left. Enormous lava flows make the fairway look like a tiny green funnel. The 6th is the most famous of Mauna Lani's par threes. It plays 202 yards across the Pacific to a green trapped on all sides. Simply one of the most beautiful golf holes in the world.

The lava flows on the back nine holes are called "pahoehoe" and have a different quality than the front. As a result the fairways are a bit more rolling. The 10th is a four par of 428 yards with a relatively broad, tree-lined fairway. The 11th is a short par five of 518 yards more or less straightaway, though it does bend slightly left at the end. The green is magnificently situated on the ocean. You must fly a bunker short of the green to roll on in two. The green of the 415-yard, dogleg left 12th hole is set in the midst of a kiawe grove. Fairway bunkers here protect you from going long and right. The 13th is a stunning hole through a valley of kiawe with lava cliffs rising on either side. The well-bunkered green is surrounded by a wall of black lava.

Day in and day out, the 16th is the toughest hole on the golf course. It plays 444 yards, frequently into the wind, to a green set against a lava cliff. The 17th hole is just 140 yards, but it's all lava rock (including the one in the middle of the bunker) and sand. The 18th doglegs left 412 yards with a cliff along the entire right side. The green sits next to the King's Trail.

Even in two halves, this is one of the most majestic courses in the world.

The par three 6th is the best known of Mani Lani's stunning short holes. It carries 202 yards over crashing ocean waves.

Pasatiempo
California

We're all fortunate to have Pasatiempo. Most of us never get to play Cypress Point or Augusta National. We only read about Royal Melbourne. But in the foothills of the Santa Cruz mountains we can all experience a little bit of the genius of Alister Mackenzie.

The Pasatiempo Golf Club has a rich and lively history. It was founded by Marion Hollins, the 1921 winner of the United States Women's Amateur Championship. Hollins worked for Samuel F.B. Morse, the builder of Pebble Beach. She became acquainted with Mackenzie when he fashioned Cypress Point. In fact there is a story, believe it if you will, that is was Hollins' ability to drive the ball over a certain oft-photographed chasm on the craggy coast that convinced Mackenzie he could build Cypress Point's famous 16th.

A fortuitous investment gave Hollins the wherewithal to build her own sports retreat—Pasatiempo. She engaged Mackenzie to design the golf course, and it will tell you something of her stature in the game that the ceremonial first foursome in 1929 was comprised of Hollins, Glenna Collett (later Vare), British champion Cyril Tolley, and a respected amateur named Robert Tyre Jones Jr. The Great Depression ended Hollins' hopes for Pasatiempo. It has survived several attempts at privatization and, fortunately, is open to us all.

When Mackenzie built Pasatiempo it was 6,845 yards with a par of 73. The present course from the championship tees only measures 6,483 yards and par is 71. Some changes have been made over the years, but enough remains of the mastery of the one of golf's greatest architects to make Pasatiempo a sheer joy.

The opening hole is 504 yards, downhill toward the harbor in Santa Cruz. It's a benign par five, with a well-bunkered green. Birdie is the objective here. Mackenzie frequently gives you room to drive the ball but very little leeway to drive the ball well. The 442-yard 2nd is a

The 9th is an uphill dogleg right par five playing to a heavily bunkered green. The harbor at Santa Cruz is in the distance.

good example. The green has a narrow opening. This is probably a harder hole than the 1st.

The 6th—where Mackenzie built his home—is a 521-yard par five with out of bounds and trees lining both sides of the fairway. The fascinating 7th is only 346 and not as tight as it looks. It actually opens up some the further out you go. Go ahead, hit the driver. The short pitch will help on this very difficult green. The 9th, back uphill to the clubhouse, is a sweet little dogleg right par five of 478 yards. There's out of bounds on the left and trees on the right off the tee, but a perfectly placed drive past the corner will put you in position to at least reach the greenside bunkers in two.

The 10th used to be a five par that required a huge carry to clear the barranca. Today it's a demanding par four of 444. A giant eucalyptus tree guards the front right of the green.

Mackenzie's favorite par four was Pasatiempo's 16th. It plays 395 with a second shot downhill, across a barranca to a triple-tiered green. The narrow 17th hole takes careful placement off the tee while the 18th provides an unusual finish—a three par of 173 yards across a cavernous barranca. Beware the pines on the right.

Maybe it's not Cypress Point, but it is a little slice of genius.

Pebble Beach
California

Pebble Beach's 18th is considered by many to be the finest finishing hole in all the world. Playing along Carmel Bay, it's certainly one of the most beautiful.

The tiny par three 7th can be anything from a sandwedge to a 2-iron depending on the wind.

The rolling par five 6th can be a pussycat unless the wind is howling.

Pebble Beach. You can count on the fingers of one hand the golf courses in the world that can rival it. Jack Neville and Douglas Grant get most of the credit, but as the saying goes, it was God that designed Pebble Beach.

Everyone knows the "book" on Pebble. You have to get it early. If you don't get ahead of this golf course, it tightens like a noose around your neck, drawing tighter and tighter. That's on a good day. If the wind is blowing a gale off Carmel Bay and the Pacific Ocean, survival is the only objective.

Weather stories are legend at Pebble Beach, some of which may even be true. Most of them involve the tiny 7th, a 107-yard par three that plays directly toward the bay. Jack Nicklaus says he has hit everything on this hole from a sandwedge to a 2-iron. One story is told about the unfortunate touring pro who tried to hit driver there into a hurricane-force wind only to have it abate in the down-swing, leaving him to helplessly watch his ball fly the tiny putting surface by some 150 yards.

The 8th, 9th, and 10th holes are the heart of Pebble Beach and comprise the toughest stretch of par fours anywhere. The 8th is a 431-yarder across a chasm to a green perched on a cliff. Next to the 17th at St. Andrews, it's probably the most famous four par in the world. The 9th and 10th, playing 464 and 426 yards respectively, stretch out on the cliff overlooking the beach at Carmel Bay.

Pebble's tournament history includes US Amateur and US Open victories there by Nicklaus and, of course, Tom Watson's dramatic victory over Nicklaus in 1982.

In fact, as you walk Pebble's fairways, think about taking the Watson test:

*Try to make a four on the 10th hole from a dicey lie on the cliffs short and right of the green.

*Hit your third shot on the magnificent 565-yard, par five 14th just off the back of the green and then try to roll a putt to a pin position on the front left. Watson made about a 50-footer here.

*Drive it into the deep bunker former USGA President Sandy Tatum had built into the dogleg on the right side of this 402-yard par four. The bunker is so deep Watson had to come out sideways. His third shot found the very back of the green. The pin was on the front. He lagged it up to within an inch.

*You may have seen something in the papers about the 17th. Watson missed the green left in the gnarly grass. He

continued

Pebble Beach, **continued**

The 464-yard 9th is one of the hardest par fours in championship golf. The 8th, 9th and 10th holes along the cliffs over the beach comprise the course's most formidable stretch.

pitched it in for a birdie two on this 209-yarder, stunning Nick-laus who had just finished ahead of him. See if you can even get it close.

*And the 18th? Out of bounds right. God's country left. Only Hale Irwin knows how to bounce it off the rocks and back into play—he did it one year to win the AT&T, alias the Crosby. The second must avoid a tree in the middle of the fairway. Watson's third was close enough to set up a birdie for a two shot win.

Don't worry if you flunk the test. Only one person ever passed it. Just take pleasure in the fact that no matter how long you'll live, you'll never play a better golf course than this one.

Imagine, if you can, Tom Watson saving a par four from the cliff ledge to the right of the 10th green.

PGA West
California

When Pete Dye signed on to build PGA West, he was challenged to create the most difficult and unusual golf course ever built. Most people agree he succeeded. Since its opening in 1986, Dye's Diabolical desert monster has been alternately cursed and blessed—but it was, from Day One, the talk of golf.

PGA West is built on a flat desert expanse that through Dye's ingenious sculpting, contouring and bunkering has become one of those rare "must-plays" on every golfer's wish list. Not withstanding occasional visits from the Bob Hope Desert Classic, the PGA West Stadium Course is best known as the happy home of the Skins Game, the made-for-TV thriller that brought us Lee Trevino's fabulous hole-in-one on the 17th and Curtis Strange's birdie

Water up the entire lefthand side makes the 440-yard 18th hole a very challenging conclusion.

from the rocks on the 10th.

If you played the PGA West Stadium Course from the very back tees it would measure 7,261 yards. But no one—no one—plays it all the way back. It's simply too difficult. Accordingly, the yardages quoted here will be from the Championship (or fourth set) of tees and not the Tournament (or suicide) tees.

The opening hole is a warmup. But, at 377 yards and with a small, contoured green, it tips you off to the prime requirement of PGA West—the tee shot must be properly placed in the fairway. The severely banked fairway bunkers are very high on the "must-avoid" list out here.

The 3rd is long and tough. The drive must avoid the fairway bunker on the left and the difficult second shot on this 446-yarder is threatened by a huge greenside bunker, also

continued

PGA West, continued.

on the left. The 4th is a tricky three par. The real danger is the deep bunker on the left, not the huge expanse of sand that runs up the right. The par five 5th is a "strategy" hole all the way. Water guards the tee ball on the left and the second shot on the right. The 7th is another short four par, where the scariest trouble is not the water front and right but the deep greenside bunker on the left.

The short 10th is where Strange learned how to balance on rocks while playing a short-iron. The 11th is the longest hole on the golf course. The sloped fairway will naturally bring anything on the right back toward the middle. The 13th is, I think, the toughest three par on the course. Play safe here and leave some air between your shot and the water. The 15th might be the toughest four par on the golf course. The fairway bunkers are fearsome.

PGA West's three closing holes are among the best known in the world. The giant 19-foot "fault" bunker to the left on the 16th green is one of the most threatening hazards in golf. The 17th is, well, Trevino's hole. At the 400-yard 18th, all you have to be is perfect. Avoid the water left and fairway bunkers right, avoid the water left on the second. Congratulations: You've seen the monster and survived.

The water on the left and the mounds on the right make the 220-yard 13th hole particularly scary.

The 11th hole is called "Eternity." At 618 yards, you can understand why.

Pinehurst
No. 2
North Carolina

Donald Ross, America's first great golf course architect, builder of Oak Hill, Seminole, Inverness, and literally hundreds of others, considered the No. 2 golf course at Pinehurst his single finest effort. During his illustrious career, Ross never quit fiddling with it—changing a tee here, a

bunker there. After Ross' death there was a brief, unenlightened period when the golf course was "modernized" by succeeding generations. Fortunately, in 1978 Tom Fazio restored much of the original design, widening fairways to bring bunkers back into play, expanding greens to recreate the subtle and challenging pin placements which had been No. 2's hallmark. The result is that Ross' No. 2 is, once again, what Ben Crenshaw termed "the finest test of chipping in the world."

Pinehurst No. 2 isn't the kind of golf course that turns your head with awe-inspiring natural beauty. There are no cliffs, no expansive valleys, no rock outcroppings, no thundering ocean waves or mountain vistas. The course is defined by sandy waste areas, majestic longleaf pine and a gently rolling terrain that, at the end of the day, has asked for and rewarded your best while, for the most part, gently forgiving your worst. And it is the best example of Ross' masterful green design that rewards only the purest plays.

There's much more to No. 2 than just the greens, however. Like the PGA World Golf Hall of Fame behind the green on the 547-yard 4th. Or the

incredibly difficult 445-yard, par four 5th which may be the best Donald Ross hole in the world. The fairway slopes right to left with out of bounds on the right. Any drive left of middle will roll down the hill, across an expanse of hardpan and into the tall pines. The perfect shot is a drive that holds the hill with a slight fade. When the pin is back left on the crowned green, only a fool shoots at it. Any miss on the left will roll down an embankment back onto the 4th fairway and wind up 60 yards away.

Tom Watson once hit driver-driver to fly it over this pin position at the 531-yard 16th.

continued

Pinehurst #2, *continued*

When you play the 578-yard 10th, think about Ben Hogan's feat there in the 1951 Ryder Cup. After hooking his drive into the woods and pitching out, Hogan launched a fairway wood 280 yards to the green and holed a 60-footer for a birdie four. Or imagine duplicating Tom Watson's eagle on the 531-yard 16th when he hit driver-driver directly over the flag and drained a 30-footer to tie Johnny Miller and go on to beat him in a playoff.

All too often some pundit declares that such-and-such a course makes you use "every club in the bag." No. 2 does that but, more importantly, it makes you use your head and your heart, too.

Bunkers and waste area guard the left side of the very difficult 5th, one of Donald Ross' finest. If the pin is back, don't shoot at it.

The 18th hole plays uphill 432 yards to a typical Donald Ross green that falls off at the edges.

The 196-yard par three 16th hole crosses a wasteland of sand to a green tucked in the pines.

Pinehurst No. 7
North Carolina

One of the things I really love about Pinehurst No. 7 is that it's Michael Jordan's favorite golf course. I mean, if you can be endorsed by America's Most Famous Avid Golfer and, arguably, the best pure athlete ever to swing a golf club, then I think you're probably doing something right. At No. 7, architect Rees Jones did an awful lot of things right.

The village of Pinehurst is a place that takes its golf and its tradition very seriously. Anytime someone

builds a course in the tall pines of the Sandhills it is invariably, immediately and unfairly compared to Ross' No. 2 masterpiece. All the more so when they both have the name "Pinehurst" attached to them. "Is it as good as No. 2?" "Does the style fit?" If someone tried to build a PGA West in Pinehurst, he'd be pilloried in the town square right in front of the Gentleman's Corner clothing store.

Pinehurst golf has an understated elegance. And, in that way, No. 7 fits the mold exactly. But don't play No. 7 looking for Donald Ross' greens. This layout is not a piece of cheap imitation. What it is, is a very, very fine Rees Jones course.

The 2nd hole might be the hardest hole in the state of North Carolina. A simple little test of 452 yards, par four, uphill and tight as a new balloon. And in case the effects of the 2nd were beginning to wear off, Jones gives you the 447-yard 6th. The tee shot plays downhill with thick woods to the left. No ball comes out of there alive. On the right is a series of mounds that can make the stance for your mid-to-long iron second shot most awkward. A very tough green, too.

The 7th is one of the cutest holes on the course. At 388 it's a layup off the tee then a short iron over some swamp/marsh/wasteland to a steeply banked green. The 530-yard 8th takes a big turn right. Don't drive it through the fairway here. The green can be reached in two but you must clear a creek to do it. The 9th is 204 over a lake that only comes into play for the most skittering, pitiful strokes.

The 12th at 546 yards is, I think, the best hole on the golf course. It narrows down to a green situated just perfectly in the land. It's a good three shot hole and one that you'll play over and over in your mind. The 13th is a lovely 203-yarder uphill, over sand and wasteland.

The 16th is the most photogenic hole in town. A good par three of 196 over wasteland. From the back tees, it presents a very difficult angle to hold the green. The par five 18th plays downhill at the end, 596 yards, water behind the green and a bunker guarding the left front. The pin always seems to be behind it.

In a town with pretty high standards, this is a course that meets all the requirements.

The Pit

North Carolina

The Pit Golf Links is built on some of the most unusual terrain you'll ever encounter. Carved out of what remains of a sand excavation, the course's more celebrated holes are characterized by ridges of craggy earth covered with scrub oak, hardy pines, and gnarled underbrush. These sandy ridges form truly formidable hazards.

The primary rule at the Pit is to keep the ball in play. At 6,600 yards from the very back tees, length is rarely a factor. But if you stray from the fairway into the sandhills and dune grass, more often than not, it means a lost ball.

There's no question that architect Dan Maples has created at the Pit some of the most uncommon holes you'll ever encounter. Some will aggravate, others will delight. But they're all memorable.

The 3rd and 4th holes will be your first experience with the Pit's unforgiving terrain. The 3rd is a tiny par four that requires a layup shot off the tee and a short iron to a sloped green guarded by dunes and thick grass left, right and front. It falls off into the woods behind. The 4th hole is a 232-yard par three, threading the needle between dunes and trees.

The 8th is a short, exacting par five with "dunes of death" on both sides all the way down the narrow fairway. This green is easily reachable in two shots but don't bother. The putting surface is tiny and runs away from you into the woods. Lay up off the tee. Lay up on your second. Try and keep your short pitch on the green. Take five and go to the next hole—which just happens to be the best on the course.

The Pit's 9th is one

The 13th hole may yield a birdie if you can make the huge carry over the water off the tee.

The tiny 16th is little more than a wedge to a very steeply sloped green. Be sure to stay below the hole on this green.

of my personal favorites anywhere in the world. It's 430 yards, dunes left and right, but the landing area is bigger than it looks. Driver (a good one) is okay here. The ingeniously contoured green is framed by a hillside covered in love grass. There are no bunkers. None are necessary. This is just a good, strong, natural golf hole.

Length comes into play on the 13th hole. A lake in front of the tee demands a huge carry to reach the fairway. Outside of the long par threes, this is the only shot on the golf course where strength rather than management is the primary requirement.

The four finishing holes put you back in the brambles, as it were, as the sandy ridges close in around you. The 15th is a par five that calls for a 3-wood or 1-iron off the tee. The second shot is a layup to the corner of the dogleg right, and the third is a short iron to a severe green. The addition of a new back tee on the 16th has lengthened the hole from what was a

silly three-quarter punch wedge to a new, improved 145-yard par three. The 17th is a dogleg left. Driver might put you through the fairway here. The 18th is a good closing hole—sort of the 530-yard par five version of the 9th.

The green on par three 4th hole is hidden away between sandhills and longleaf pines. There's more room than it would appear, though.

Sea Island
Georgia

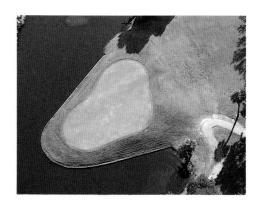

about your game.

Seaside's opening hole is 398 yards with a lone fairway bunker right and a deep bunker short and left of the green. The 2nd is 428, and you can let it out here. The 222-yard 3rd is protected by marsh up the left. The 4th is a superb hole, 377 yards across

The V-shaped green of the Plantation's 155-yard 7th hole is well protected by water.

Going to the Sea Island Golf Club is like stepping into history. The entrance to the club is through a majestic avenue of giant live oaks draped in Spanish Moss. Tabby ruins of the Retreat Plantation buildings are preserved near the clubhouse. Tabby is a mixture of sand, oyster shells, and lime used in construction like cement. Retreat Plantation existed on the tip of St. Simon's Island for almost a century beginning in 1780.

The golf courses are no less historic. The original nine holes, Plantation, was built in 1927 by Walter Travis. In 1929 the Seaside nine was added by H.S. Colt and Charles Alison. At the same time Colt and Alison reworked the Plantation nine, creating a full eighteen-hole test. Dick Wilson built the Retreat nine in 1960, and Joe Lee added the Marshside in 1973, giving Sea Island thirty-six holes in all. In keeping with the sense of Sea Island's history, however, it's the Plantation and Seaside holes we deal with here.

The Plantation is relatively short at 3,272 yards and very traditional—truly a pleasure to play. The 2nd, for example, is a dandy little 350-yard par four with a well-protected, elevated green. You have to cozy up to the fairway bunkers for the best angle. The 8th gives you plenty of room to drive the ball on this 415-yard hole, but the second shot is played to a well-bunkered green. The 9th is 471 yards and reachable in two shots if you can drive it out of the chute and into the fairway. It's a nine holes of golf that should make you feel good

marsh to a landing area with three bunkers to catch drives through the fairway. The green is guarded by two bunkers right and marsh and trees left. On the 346-yard 5th, take your tee ball over the bunker in the middle of the fairway. The green is protected in front and right by two deep bunkers. The 6th is another short par five of 472 yards. Drive in the left side of the fairway, over the bunker, and you'll get home in two. The 424-yard 7th hole requires a carry of 220 yards over marsh to reach the prime fairway position. The 8th hole plays 194 yards over a deep, fingered bunker. The 9th is another short par five. You should be able to drive it past the trouble but trees make the approach to the green as narrow as the avenue of oaks.

There's very little room to miss a shot on the 414-yard 7th hole of the Seaside. You must carry the ball 220 yards over marsh to reach the fairway.

Semiahmoo
Washington

From the fairway on the 14th, a dogleg right of 415 yards, you can see White Rock, Canada, in the distance across Drayton Harbor. The 15th hole is a 211-yard par three into a narrow green. You'll be able to see two ships, one sunken and one abandoned, left in their resting places in the bay.

Semiahmoo has a very strong finish. The 539-yard, par five 17th is reachable for only the longest hitters. The fairway bunkers on the right catch a lot of tee shots. The green is tiered with bunkers front, right and left.

The 18th is a gorgeous finishing hole and can be a severe test when it plays into the wind. The 409-yard par four has three bunkers on the left and one on the right in the landing area. A pond wraps around the green front, right and behind. A pesky lone tree protects the right side as well.

Semiahmoo is cut through dense forest. Sometimes you feel like it's just you, the deer and the eagles out there.

The Semiahmoo Golf and Country Club is hidden away on a little spit of land not far from Blaine in the northwest corner of Washington State. The site of an old Alaska Packers cannery, the resort and marina are actually located on the tiny finger of land that separates Drayton Harbor and Semiahmoo Bay. The golf course is back across Drayton Harbor just a bit, quite literally carved out of a forest of cedar and fir, alder and hemlock.

Built on an essentially flat piece of ground in 1987, this Arnold Palmer/Ed Seay creation features softly mounded fairways, rock-walled greens, and a sense of complete isolation. Virtually all the holes are encased in forest. You're more apt to see deer or even an eagle than another foursome.

From the back, or "Palmer" tees as they call them, the course is a rather stout 7,005 yards. As heavily wooded as the terrain is, the game could become a bit claustrophobic but Palmer and Seay have given you plenty of room to get, and keep, the golf ball in play.

The front nine has two exceedingly difficult four pars. The 4th hole plays 417 yards to an elevated green bunkered front and left. The slick green is sloped back to front. The 7th is a gigantic dogleg left par four of 453 yards.

The rock-walled 12th is a well-bunkered 173-yard par three. Water guards this green on three sides.

Spanish Bay
California

The Links at Spanish Bay is the combined effort of an unusual trio. Robert Trent Jones Jr. brought the course design and construction expertise while five time British Open champion Tom Watson and his old pal, Frank "Sandy" Tatum brought the "feel." The result is this magnificent, wind-swept links-style course set in the dramatic dunes hard by the Pacific Ocean.

Tatum—a respected San Francisco lawyer, former NCAA golf champion, and a past president of the United States Golf Association— has been a fast friend of Watson's since Tom was a student at Stanford. They've been known to travel to Scotland together the week before the British Open just to get in a few rounds on some of the great links courses.

Spanish Bay is dedicated to the proposition of bringing links golf to America. The ocean and the wind were already there. But the ingredient frequently missing in American seaside courses is the firmness of ground and openings to greens that allow a player to run the ball under the wind. In an effort to give Spanish Bay that hard, fast quality, fescue grass was used. It has proved a mixed blessing. Maintaining the fescue turned out to be

Deep Scottish-style pot bunkers add an authentic links touch to this wild seaside course.

more difficult than anyone thought it would be. Still, Spanish Bay is probably the closest thing to true "links" golf that exists on this continent.

You'll get the idea right out of the blocks. The 1st hole is a short, 500-yard par five that turns slightly right at the end and plays directly toward the ocean. It can be an easy birdie or, if the wind is up, it can be the beginning of a perilous adventure.

The short 2nd will play with the prevailing winds. At 307 can you drive it? Is it worth the risk? No. The 5th is a big par four of 459 that sweeps right toward the sea. The three fairway bunkers must be avoided here. The gutsy play is a blind drive over a dune, carrying the bunker on the right. The 6th is a downwind four par of 395 with scads of bunkers protecting the dogleg. It's the first of six holes that plays along the 17 Mile Drive.

On only three holes—the 10th, 11th and 12th tucked back in the Monterey pines—do you lose sight of the

continued

continued

The 200-yard par three 16th green at Spanish Bay is virtually on the beach.

Spanish Bay, continued

ocean. The 13th is a three par into the wind of only 126 yards. The greens at Spanish Bay are very, very difficult. If you hadn't noticed that yet, you'll figure it out here.

Coming in, the 14th and the 17th are my favorites. The former is a wicked and splendid 571-yard par five. It plays into the wind and the second shot is threatened by a huge bunker in the middle of the fairway, another smaller one right and two left. A great three-shot hole. The 17th only plays parallel the beach—a gaggle of bunkers on the right guard the tee shot on this 414-yarder. The greenside bunker is long and left. The wind will be coming hard across right to left. The 18th makes a superb finisher. It's 571 yards but so narrow you can't play it after meals.

Spanish Bay might be the newcomer on the peninsula but in a way, it's as old as golf itself.

The wildflowers can be lovely unless you have to look for your ball in them.

The 18th is a 571-yard par five with an approach

over a natural wetland to a very undulating green.

Of course, you could say that about nearly all the greens.

Spyglass Hill
California

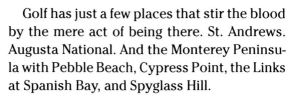

Golf has just a few places that stir the blood by the mere act of being there. St. Andrews. Augusta National. And the Monterey Peninsula with Pebble Beach, Cypress Point, the Links at Spanish Bay, and Spyglass Hill.

Monterey is a magic place. The craggy cypress trees cling to the rock cliffs. The otters tread water out in Carmel Bay. And the weather is pure Scotland, while just a few miles inland it might be pure California. The tiny town of Carmel isn't quaint—it's the boutique capital of the world. It's best known pub, the Hog's Breath Inn, is owned by Clint Eastwood. And it seems like there are more art galleries than parking spaces. The golf, though, is oh so very divine.

Spyglass Hill is a Robert Trent Jones creation added to the peninsula's delights in 1966. It's named in honor of Carmel's most famous resident. No, not Clint Eastwood or Bing Crosby—Robert Louis Stevenson. The holes bear names like "Treasure Island," "Billy Bones," "Long John Silver," "Admiral Benbow," and so on. But the pleasure of the fantasy is in the playing.

continued

Spyglass Hill's opening holes weave through the dunes along the shore.

Spyglass' spectacular 4th, called "Blind Pew", sits amidst the seaside dunes.

Spyglass Hill, Continued.

Some critics claim that Spyglass Hill uses its most dramatic land in the first few holes. I prefer to think of it as putting its best foot forward. There is no getting around the fact that Spyglass' first five holes are among the most beautiful in the world.

The opener runs downhill 600 yards toward the ocean and, consequently, into the prevailing winds. The next four holes are all nestled in the dunesland, buffeted by the ocean breezes. The 2nd is a short four par of only 350 yards uphill across the dunes to a bunkerless, but hardly defenseless, green. The 3rd is a stunning par three of 150 yards, again across dunes toward the sea. The 4th is 365 yards surrounded by sand and dune grass. The 5th is the last seaside hole, a 180-yarder playing into a quartering wind.

Now it's time to put the camera away and get down to business. The 415-yard 6th begins the trip back uphill where Spyglass plays itself out in a forest of tall Monterey pines. Every hole seems narrow and threatening. Wilderness left, wilderness right. And devilish hazards in between.

Monterey Pines line the fairway of the 515-yard 7th, known as "Indian Village."

The par three 12th presents a very small target, indeed. That's why it's called "Skeleton Island."

Tanglewood Park
North Carolina

The second shot to the dogleg right 439-yard 18th is decidedly uphill to a heavily bunkered and well-contoured green.

Not all of North Carolina's great golf courses are in the tall pines of the sandhills or the coastal marshes. One of Carolina's finest is tucked into the hills and valleys of red clay tobacco country west of Winston-Salem. It's Tanglewood Park built by Robert Trent Jones in 1958.

Tanglewood was the name given to the 1,200-acre country estate of W.N. Reynolds, a member of the Reynolds tobacco family. After Reynolds' death in 1951, the trustees converted it into a public park, which today has two golf courses, a tennis center, and equestrian facilities with boarding and training areas and bridle trails. More to the point, Tanglewood has one of the great public golf courses in the country. The Championship Course is the annual host of the Vantage Senior Championship, the richest event on the PGA Senior Tour by some considerable margin. It was also the site of the 1974 PGA Championship won by Lee Trevino by one stroke over Jack Nicklaus.

When Tanglewood was originally constructed it was a pleasant little, 6,500-yard country tester. Then the PGA decided to visit, and Jones was called in to lengthen and strengthen it. He increased the yardage from 6,500 to 7,048 while reducing the par from 72 to 70. The size of the greens was trimmed back about twenty percent. Roughly forty-five bunkers were added to the sixty-five already on the course.

A few additional changes have been made at Tanglewood. The nines have been flopped from the order of play in the 1974 PGA. Also, the 3rd and 11th holes have been stretched into short par fives of 470 and 490 yards, respectively, restoring par on the course to 72. And in 1989 nearly one million dollars was spent refurbishing all eighteen greens and many of the fairways, making Tanglewood as well conditioned as it is well designed.

Tanglewood can seem like a sea of bunkers, but nowhere more so than the demanding finishing holes of both nines. The front finish begins with the 243-yard downhill 7th—a bunker and pond left and two bunkers right. The 8th is only 440, dogleg left to a large green surrounded by bunkers while the 9th (where Trevino two-putted from above the hole to best Nicklaus in '74) is 439 with an uphill second to a green steeply sloped back to front.

The three-hole finale is not as tough as the last three holes on the front. Still, these can be treacherous if you need to gamble. The 16th is 183 yards with nothing but a flagstick and bunkers in sight. The green is among the toughest on the course. The 17th is 535 yards and can be reached in two but the long second shot has to carry a giant cross bunker and a couple of greenside bunkers. The dogleg right 439-yard 18th is a very difficult driving hole with bunkers guarding the dogleg. The second shot is so uphill it's almost blind. The green is protected by a deep bunker in the right front and bunkers all around the back.

Chances are you'll find more sand at Tanglewood Park than in the sandhills themselves.

The green on the downhill 364-yard 10th is surrounded with four large bunkers. With 110 bunkers on the course, nearly every green is encircled with sand.

Two long bunkers run up either side of the green on the par five 11th. At 490 yards it's reachable and a good birdie opportunity.

Teton Pines
Wyoming

There's nothing quite like Jackson, Wyoming. The sidewalks are wooden and the saloons still have swinging doors. There are covered wagon trips, stagecoach rides, and rodeos. Nearby, there is whitewater rafting on the Snake River and the singular beauty of of Yellowstone National Park and the Grand Tetons.

Two magnificent golf courses can also be found. The Jackson Hole Golf and Tennis Club is north of town near the Gros Ventre River. To the west, across the Snake River and nearer the mountains, is Teton Pines—where Arnold Palmer and Ed Seay built a magnificent, 7,401 monster.

Even taking the altitude into consideration, Teton Pines is a big golf course. It's set in an open valley dotted with wildflowers and decorated with stands of aspen and pine. The Grand Tetons are the backdrop, but when you're playing Teton Pines, the water is the more immediate concern.

Teton Pines opens with a 444-yard par four backed up by a 609-yard par five. There are two terrific three pars on the front nine. The 3rd hole is 204 yards with a giant bunker short and left and water on the right. The 8th is 170 yards, total carry over the lake from island tee boxes.

The Grand Tetons peak over a ridge alongside the 412-yard 11th.

The 10th is one of the most unusual holes in the world. In order to prevent two creeks from merging (and infringing on all-important water rights) one creek crosses another over an aqueduct in front of the tee. The 572-yard par five continues to play between the creeks in a double-dogleg.

The 333-yard 17th is another ingenious hole and the shortest par four on the course. The tee shot is threatened by water all along the right and requires deft placement. Another finger of water cuts across in front of the diagonally set green. The finishing hole is a big dogleg right of 472 yards with water right, fairway bunker left, and bunkers protecting each side of the green.

The green on the 437 yard 9th hole is built into a grove of Aspens. The gold leaves make for a gorgeous setting in the autumn.

Tidewater
South Carolina

Not all great golf courses are designed by well-known architects. In fact, some of the greatest courses in the United States were built by people whose only qualification was an abiding love of the game. The Tidewater Golf Club in North Myrtle Beach falls into that category.

For decades South Carolina's Grand Strand has been a golfer's dream destination. Tidewater makes it even more so. The course is the maiden project of Ken Tomlinson, a lawyer turned architect. It's built on a peninsula between the Intracoastal Waterway and the saltmarshes near an Atlantic Ocean inlet. The front nine has two holes near the Cherry Grove Ocean Inlet and two holes along the waterway. The back nine features two more holes along the inlet and three additional holes on the waterway. The inland holes are carved through thick forest.

The 3rd hole is the first par three with a view of the ocean inlet. It's only 150 yards, but there are bunkers front and back right and saltmarsh all along the left. The 4th is a terrific 420-yard par four along the marsh. It's a very difficult driving hole and the green is surrounded by bunkers but it's a beauty.

The 12th is Tidewater's signature hole, a 180-yarder to a bulkheaded green with the ocean in the distance. The 545-yard 13th gets my vote as the best hole on the course. With the saltmarshes (and the Atlantic) all the way on the right and woods on the left, it's a stunning golf hole. The 14th is a huge par four of 460 yards with the second across a pond. It's not as fearsome as it sounds but every bit as long.

The two closing holes are as tough a finish as you'll find on the Strand. The 17th is a 210-yarder across the marsh along the Intracoastal. The 18th is a paltry 440 yards with marsh all the way along the right. All it takes is perfection—which is close to what this course is.

Tidewater's 2nd hole, bunkered heavily on the right, is cut through a virgin forest.

The 4th hole is a demanding 420 yard par four along the marsh. It's tough getting the ball in play here.

Tokatee
Oregon

Tall Douglas fir trees and the snow-capped Three Sisters provide the setting for Tokatee.

There are some places that simply make you want to throw the bag over your shoulder and go play. Tokatee Golf Club is one of those.

Tucked away in the tall Douglas firs with the snow-covered Three Sisters rising above the distant horizon, this is the kind of place that makes memories.

Ted Robinson, a well-respected golf course architect in the Pacific Northwest but little-known outside it, laid out a spectacular course that seems suited to that exact purpose. There are no five-mile cart rides from the green to the next tee. This vintage 1966 course is laid out in the style of the old masters. It's also a thoroughly delightful and challenging 6,817-yard test.

The 2nd is among the most demanding holes, a long four par of 433 yards to a green bunkered front left and back right. The 3rd hole is a 567-yard par five with several large trees puckishly guarding avenues of access in the fairway. The 5th again has a tall fir tree blocking the entrance to the green.

On the back the 10th is a long, tree-lined par four of 419 yards. The fairway slopes right toward the trees and jail. The 376-yard 15th should provide a good chance at a birdie while the 16th is an ingenious 532-yard three-shotter. It plays directly toward the Three Sisters and a creek crosses the fairway about 325 yards off the tee. Further up, the fairway narrows with a pond left and trees right. It's possible to get home in two but risky.

Tokatee closes with a pretty par three of 152 yards over water and the gently curving 412-yard 18th. Just your average idyllic day in the Cascades.

The 204-yard 11th plays across water to a green protected by water on the right and a bunker left.

Torrey Pines
California

The 158-yard third hole plays downhill and toward the Pacific. Here the wind is in your face and the hang-gliders launch themselves from the cliffs to your left.

Built along cliffs that tower over the Pacific Ocean, Torrey Pines' South Course north of San Diego is perhaps the finest municipal golf course in North America. Playing the holes overlooking the Pacific in the golden late afternoon light, one can't help but be captivated by the natural beauty of this spot.

Designed in the 1950s by William P. Bell, Torrey Pines South and its companion North Course are the site of the PGA Tour's San Diego Open. It's generally acknowledged that the 7,021-yard South is several shots tougher than the equally lovely North layout. But when the wind blows hard off the ocean, beauty becomes secondary to the challenge.

Torrey Pines' South doesn't waste any time letting you know exactly what's in store. The 1st hole is a big 453-yard par four that plays directly toward the ocean. The South's trademark is that the longest, most demanding holes are made all the more difficult because they play into the prevailing winds. Par is a very good beginning.

The 4th might be the prettiest hole on the golf course. It plays along the cliff overlooking the beach and the ocean. And, yes, that is a nude beach down there. Keep your mind on your game, though. This 447-yard par four with cliffs left and trouble right requires all your attention.

The 7th is another of Torrey Pines' monster four pars. It doglegs right 454 yards back into the wind. The 469-yard 12th is a par four and a half. It's into the wind all the way. The 14th and 15th turn toward home with relatively short par fours. You may recognize the tree on the 14th where Craig Stadler played his famous "towel" shot.

The final three holes make for a great finish. The 16th is 201 yards, usually into a quartering wind. The 426-yard 17th has cliffs on the left side, and the 499-yard 18th is reachable in two shots with a very good drive. Anything less, though, and you must lay-up short of "Devlin's Billabong" with a mid-iron. In 1975, it took Bruce Devlin six attempts from there to find the putting surface. Don't let it be your billabong, too.

Torrey Pines South's 13th is a 533 yard par five over a rolling fairway. If the wind is at your back, which it frequently is, it's possible to get home in two.

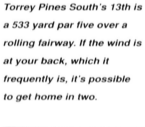

TPC at Sawgrass

Florida

No golf course has ever been put under the microscope quite like Pete Dye's Tournament Players Club. From the time the first bulldozer moved on this piece of Ponte Vedra swampland, this was to be the permanent site of the PGA Tour's own championship. It was to be the showcase, the conversation piece, maybe even provide the missing link between the Tour and a major championship.

From the very first day the pros screamed. Almost unanimously, they praised its routing, shot selection, and strategic qualities. And just as unanimously they berated the greens, deeming them too small, bumpy, quirky, and undulating. Since that first year when Jerry Pate finished birdie-birdie to win by 2 and threw both PGA Tour commissioner Deane Beman and Dye into the pond along the 18th, every green has been recontoured—or perhaps I should say *de*contoured.

What's left, though, is still one of the great tests of golf anywhere. One of Dye's design tenets is that a golf course should look harder than it actually is. I'm not sure he succeeded at the Players Club because this golf course is every bit as hard as it looks.

Often imitated, the short 17th hole at The Players Club is the most famous island green in the world. And the scariest.

The 5th is probably the toughest par on the golf course. The 454-yard par four requires a solid drive in the fairway (there's waste area right and swales left) and then a long iron into a large green protect-

ed on the left by a bunker and trees and the right by mounds.

The opening nine has a tough finish with the 215-yard 8th and the 582-yard 9th. The latter is a superb three-shot par five calling for a good drive, a well placed second and a precise short iron to a tricky green.

The 11th is an ingenious go or no-go par five. It has a huge, rolling putting surface protected by a gigantic 80 or 90-yard bunker and water on the right, pot bunkers, and swales on the left.

The finish is pure Pete Dye genius. The 16th is a 497-yard par five. Reachable but terrifying with water right and behind. Let's talk terror for a minute. Add a bit of wind to the famous island green on the 132-yard 17th and that's what you get, pure knee-knocking terror. The 440-yard 18th is only one of the best final holes in golf. There's water left, but favor the right too much and you wind up on the spectator mounds or blocked by trees. The terraced green is guarded by grass bunkers right and water left. And, remember, this is the easy version.

The 18th curves left around a lake. With water left and mounds right, it's a very difficult driving hole. The second shot is no bargain, either.

TPC
at
Scottsdale
Arizona

Just to the north of the Tournament Players Club at Scottsdale, Jay Morrish and Tom Weiskopf built Troon and Troon North through the rocks and rolling terrain, the centuries-old saguaro cacti, and Pinnacle Peak. It was gorgeous, rich, desert land, and they used it cleverly. No such option existed at the TPC Scottsdale.

The land was quite literally a waste area. A bit of tumbleweed and a snake or two comprised the limited flora and fauna. It was little more than a dike for Scottsdale and Phoenix down the hill from the high desert—something to keep the populace from being flooded out in the occasional gully washer. Part of what makes this municipally owned TPC course so interesting is that it was a complete creation of the imagination, one that year in and year out is praised for its shot values and playability by the PGA Tour's players.

When Weiskopf and Morrish routed the holes much of the area in between, with the exception of the spectator mounds, was

restored to desert terrain. The look of the land today is of winding ribbons of fairway and dramatic grassy mounds surround by stark, dusty desert.

The 554-yard 3rd is a brilliant three-shot par five with a fairway bunker in the left landing area and a gully and hazard running up the right side,

The 12th is a 200-yard par three with water behind and right, bunkers and desert left.

The green of the 515-yard par five 15th is an island. It can be reached in two but only by the most courageous.

then crossing in front of the green. You must carefully pick a spot among seven fairway bunkers to nestle your second shot. The 5th hole tees off from the back door of the Scottsdale Princess resort. It's a 453-yard par four. There is desert on both sides and a hazard that crosses the fairway short of the green but it is length that makes this hole so difficult.

The 9th hole is a pretty par four with three fairway bunkers and spectator mounds along the right side. A deep bunker in the front middle divides the large green. There's a bunker right and an embankment left.

The finish at the TPC Scottsdale has already earned a well-deserved reputation for excitement. The 15th is a clas-sic go/no-go par five. The drive on this 501-yard hole has water along the left and desert right. The green is surrounded by water with bunkers right and left. It's reachable but the sensible move for mere mortals is to lay up. The 16th is a terrific 162-yard par three with deep bunkers and an undulating green. The 17th is only 332 and can be driven, but there is a deep pot bunker short in the middle of the fairway that must be cleared—a great gambling hole.

The 18th has already seen its share of disasters. The water along the left invites you to cut off as much as you can. Take it at the fairway bunker on the right and turn it over. A deep bunker protects the large green on the right.

Amazing what the right people can make out of nothing.

A lot of high hopes have drowned in the water along the left side of the 18th fairway. Aim for the fairway bunker and turn it over.

Troon North
Arizona

*The 10th hole only measures
392 yards so play an iron
off the tee short of the fairway
bunker. From there it's
a short iron over the desert to
a very undulating green.*

A chance encounter with Tom Weiskopf one afternoon gave me the opportunity to tell him how much I admired his golf course at Troon. I told him it was the best "modern" course I had ever seen. He politely thanked me and then asked if I had seen his new course, Troon North. "A lot of people seem to like it even more," he said without the slightest hint of braggadocio.

It's nearly beyond comprehension that within a couple of miles of each other Jay Morrish, in collaboration with Weiskopf, could create two such brilliant designs. Thankfully for all of us, one of them is entirely open to the public. And Weiskopf didn't exaggerate it's masterfulness, either.

Troon North makes two loops through the high Sonoran Desert foothills above Scottsdale. It threads its bright green fairways through saguaro cactus, arroyos, and enormous piles of dust brown boulders. Playing in the desert for the first time can be very intimidating. The areas off the golf course look so foreboding that it's easy to be intimidated standing on the tee. The desert is so penal, though, that most architects—and specifically Morrish and Weiskopf—give you ample room to drive the golf ball. Troon North has the additional advantage of some banking on the outside edges of the fairways and rough areas that tend to kick the slightly off-line shots back into the playing area.

The 176-yard 13th plays across the desert to a green guarded front and back by bunkers.

The course plays to 7,008-yards from the black (back) tees. And there isn't a weak hole out there. The 3rd is a unique 544-îyard dogleg right with a huge boulder in the fairway at the corner. The green is a figure eight with a swale in the middle. The 4th is 420 requiring a somewhat intimidating tee shot over what seems like an endless expanse of boulders. The 5th is a great hole. It's 464 with a sloping, contoured fairway. The green is a narrow target with no bunkers, just a deep swale on the left that has double-bogey written all over it.

The little 10th might be the prettiest hole on the course. It's a long iron off the tee, laying up short of the far bunker. Then it's a short iron over wash, boulders, and wasteland to a heavily contoured green. The 11th is 539 and it tightens up all the way to the narrow green, protected by a boulder mountain left and desert wash right.

The 15th tee on this downhill 368-yarder will give you a view of the desert you won't soon forget. The 16th is a nifty 140-yard par three. The interestingly shaped and contoured green has big bunkers left and right. The shot plays over desert, boulders, wash, and a pond.

The course finishes with two challenging par fours. The 17th is 438 with an undulating fairway and another bunkerless green guarded by a deep swale. The 18th is a 444-yard dogleg left to a green that sweeps steeply from back to front. The distant back is the practice putting green.

Tryall
West Indies

The 434-yard 14th is downhill and frequently into the wind. It's a great view from the top of the hill, though.

The Great Houses of Jamaica are stone-and-mortar relics of colonial days, archeological proof of the enormous wealth of the sugar cane plantations. Some of the stone mansions have been destroyed by hurricanes, others razed well over a century ago in the slave uprisings. A few survive as museums, a private residence or two or, as in the case of the great house at Tryall, as a hotel and resort.

The Tryall Great House sits atop a hill that seems about a thousand steps above the Caribbean beach. It holds a commanding view of the sea west of Montego Bay along Jamaica's northern shore —the "resort" coast. The sugar cane plantation disappeared long ago, though the giant water wheel behind the 6th tee is a remnant. In time coconut palms replaced sugar cane as Tryall's cash crop. In turn, the coconuts were replaced by tourists lodging in the Great House and investors who built luxurious villas in the hillside rising above the Great House. Ralph Plummer, an architect of a couple of Texas courses you've probably heard of—Preston Trail and Champions, was imported to build a golf course at the bottom of the hill.

Tryall plays just 6,407 yards from the back tees to a par of 71. But when the wind howls off the ocean, it can be a definite struggle. The 545-yard 3rd is a par five that sweeps left. A pond threatens the second so keep it to the right. The green is hard by the Caribbean and protected by four bunkers—a three-shot hole into the wind. The 4th tee is almost on the beach. The hole is a slight dogleg left of 340 yards. The 5th is another good par five of 512 yards. You can reach the water hazard on the right from the tee. The green is protected by four bunkers and water up the right side of the fairway but it can be reached in two shots.

Across the road, the 6th is a 398-yard uphill par four. The drive should be left here because the fairway slopes back to the right. The 7th hole is just 138 yards but the green is heavily bunkered. The Great House is above on the hill to your left. Don't stand under the coconut palms for shade—you may develop a sudden and excruciating headache. The 8th hole is a 395-yard par four dogleg right to an elevated green. A drainage ditch, which plays as a hazard, crosses in front of the green. It's a tough little four.

The 9th is a big dogleg left par four of 436 yards. The second shot is all uphill—the second-hardest par on the golf course.

The view from the 14th tee is why you came to Jamaica. It's also the hardest hole on the golf course, playing 434 yards downhill but into the wind. The green falls off to oblivion on the right.

You go back across the road for the final two holes. The 17th is a 402-yard par four with the green protected by a ditch in front. The 18th is a relatively easy finishing hole, just 338 yards but with a well-bunkered green and out of bounds and plenty of beach to the left.

The green of the 545 -yard third hole backs right up to the Caribbean. Not much chance of getting home in two here.

Ventana Canyon
Arizona

The Sonoran desert with its sentries of ancient saguaro cacti has beckoned nearly every modern-day golf course architect. Ventana Canyon, tucked in the foothills of the Santa Catalina Mountains near Tucson, is Tom Fazio's magnificent offering. The Canyon Course is a stunning and difficult desert delight that plays 6,818 yards through desert, wash, boulders, cactus, jackrabbits, coyote, and canyons.

After a fairly relaxing start, you enter the breathtaking Esperrero Canyon from the third tee. The shot on the 401-yard hole is a 1-iron or 3-wood from a cliff to a fairway with bunkers and desert on the right and a creek on the left. The second shot plays dramatically downhill, though it doesn't appear that way. The green is bunkered on both sides and will not hold anything too bold. Guard against going over here.

The 5th is the last hole in the Esperrero but it's a beauty. It's a 148-yard par three entirely over desert to a kidney-shaped green. There are pot bunkers and desert to the right and a creek to the left. The ideal shot is to the right side of the green, allowing the ball to trickle back toward the pin.

The back nine is as strong as any nine holes in the desert. The 10th is a downhill, 336-yard par four with trees and desert on the right and desert on the left. Find the left side of the fairway with a long iron or 3-wood. The Whaleback Rock, a gargantuan boulder, sits behind the green and can come into play if you are forced to carry the large greenside bunker on the right. The 11th hole plays 463

Ventana Canyon's 13th hole is a dangerous par three of just 158 yards but, as you can tell, you best not miss the green here.

yards downhill with bunkers on the left and desert right. Anything on the left side of the fairway will feed back toward the middle. The second shot is much more severely downhill than it looks. Make yourself take less club. From the right side of the green the ball will roll down toward the hole.

The Canyon Course boasts a very strong finish beginning with the downhill, 474-yard par four 15th. The hole doglegs left with the second shot playing back uphill to a green that drops off into a hazard on the left and desert on the right. The 16th is a 221-yard par three, uphill with desert left and grass bunkers and mounds on the right. The 17th is a 442-yard, uphill, dogleg right par four with a trio of fairway bunkers at the corner. You have to stay to the left to be able to see the green. The 18th is a superb finishing hole. It's a 503-yard, dogleg right five par with desert right and bunkers left off the tee. Favor the left. There's a desert wash that crosses in front of the green with more desert on the left, water right and a waterfall behind. It's possible to get home in two but the smart play is to lay-up. And the first rule in the desert is: Play smart, there's trouble out there you don't even want to know about.

The 17th is an uphill, dogleg right 442-yard par four that plays toward the Santa Catalina Mountains.

Wild
Dunes
South Carolina

After Hurricane Hugo registered a direct hit on Charleston in 1989, Wild Dunes was quite a sight. The golf course was a maze of uprooted oaks. Pine trees were twisted in the middle and then snapped off or bent over like cornstalks after the harvest. By the ocean, the 18th was covered with sand and beach debris. The tee box was gone. Behind it the entire 17th hole had just disappeared. About all that was left was a piece of drainage pipe sticking out of what used to be a piece of the green. The 18-foot water surge had erased one of the prettiest holes on the East Coast.

Since it opened in 1980, Tom Fazio's Wild Dunes Links Course has been internationally acclaimed, made famous to a large measure, by its stunning ocean finish. It took a year to rebuild but the 17th and 18th holes have been restored, even improved somewhat, as difficult as that might be to imagine.

The Links Course begins in inland South Carolina. The new 3rd hole was lengthened around 30 yards to 432, bringing the fairway bunker guarding the corner of the dogleg more into play. An oak protects the entrance to the green. New teeing ground was also added at the 421-yard 6th.

The back nine begins through rolling sandhills. The short 10th is only 331 yards but tight and dangerous. The 376-yard 11th with a single bunker behind the green is similar. The key is keeping the ball in play through this stretch. The 192-yard 12th plays downhill to a green set in a dune. The 427-yard 13th is a tough dogleg left playing to a green in the next dune over. Miss left and you're in the deep dune grasses and underbrush, miss right and roll down the hill to face a nearly impossible pitch.

The 15th is an underrated hole on the course. It plays 426 with hazard and marsh on the left and fairway bunkers on the right. The 175-yard 16th has marsh and hazard along the rightside.

Now, to the classic finish. The new 17th is about 30 yards longer, measuring 409 yards. The tee on the par five 540-yard 18th has been shifted 10 yards to the right and elevated, giving the player a better view of the deep pot bunker guarding the fairway and the dogleg. Originally a series of dunes separated the 17th and 18th fairways from the ocean. The hurricane, of course, swept those away. The 18th fairway is now virtually adjacent to the beach. At high tide you could hook it into the water.

With time and wind, the dunes will come back. Fortunately, the golf course already has.

Devastated by Hurricane Hugo, the magnificent 540-yard 18th and the dunes alongside it have been rebuilt and, surprisingly, improved. A higher tee box on the 18th yields a better view of the hole.

The 12th is a 192-yard downhill par three set back in the sand dunes. You don't want to miss this green.

140

CONTACT INFORMATION

Call or write the following courses for specific information. (Contact information was correct at time of compilation; the publishers are not responsible for subsequent changes.)

ARROWHEAD GOLF CLUB:
10850 W. Sundown Trail, Littleton, CO 80125; (303) 973-4076

BANFF SPRINGS:
P.O. Box 960, Banff, Alberta, Canada T0L 0C0; (403) 762-2211

BARTON CREEK RESORT AND COUNTRY CLUB:
8212 Barton Club Dr., Austin, TX 78735; (800) 527-3220

BETHPAGE BLACK, BELMONT LAKE STATE PARK:
P.O. Box 247, Babylon, NY 11702; (516) 249-0700

BLACKWOLF RUN:
1111 West Riverside Dr., Kohler, WI 53044; (414) 457-4446

THE BOULDERS:
34631 North Tom Darlington Dr., Carefree, AZ 85377; (602) 488-9009

BOYNE HIGHLANDS:
Harbor Springs, MI 49740; (616) 549-2441

BRECKENRIDGE GOLF CLUB:
200 Clubhouse Dr., Breckenridge, CO 80424; (303) 453-9104

THE BROADMOOR GOLF CLUB:
Colorado Springs, CO 80906; (719) 634-7711

CANTIGNY:
27W270 Mack Rd., Wheaton, IL 60187; (312) 668-3323

CARAMBOLA BEACH RESORT & GOLF CLUB:
P.O. Box 3031, Kingshill, St. Croix, US Virgin Islands 00851; (809) 778-3800

CASA DE CAMPO:
La Romana, Dominican Republic; (809) 523-3333

COG HILL GOLF & COUNTRY CLUB:
119th & Archer Ave., Lemont, IL 60439; (708) 257-5872

CONCORD RESORT HOTEL:
Kiamesha Lake, NY 12751; (914) 794-4000

DESERT DUNES:
19300 Palm Dr., Palm Springs, CA 92263; (619) 329-2941

DESERT INN COUNTRY CLUB:
3145 Las Vegas Blvd. S., Las Vegas, NV 89109; (702) 733-4290

DORAL HOTEL & COUNTRY CLUB:
4400 Northwest 87th Ave., Miami, FL 33178; (305) 592-2000

EDGEWOOD TAHOE:
P.O. Box 5400, Stateline, NV 89449; (702) 588-2787

GLEN ABBEY GOLF COURSE:
1333 Dorval Dr., Oakville, Ontario, Canada L6J 4Z3; (416) 844-1800

GRAND CYPRESS:
One N. Jacaranda, Orlando, FL 32819; (407) 239-4700

GRAND TRAVERSE RESORT:
Grand Traverse Village, MI 49610; (616) 938-2100

THE GREENBRIER:
White Sulphur Springs, W VA 24986; (304) 536-1110

HARBOUR TOWN GOLF LINKS:
11 Lighthouse Lane, Hilton Head Island, SC 29928; (803) 671-2446

HEATHER GLEN:
Hwy. 17 North, North Myrtle Beach, SC 29597; (803) 249-9000

HERITAGE PLANTATION:
P.O. Box 2010, Pawleys Island, SC 29585; (803) 237-3424

THE HOMESTEAD:
Rt. 3, Hot Springs, VA 24445; (703) 839-5660

HOMINY HILL GOLF COURSE:
Mercer Road, Colts Neck, NJ 07722; (201) 462-9222

HORSESHOE BAY COUNTRY CLUB RESORT:
P.O. Box 7766, Horseshoe Bay, TX 78654; (512) 598-2511

INNISBROOK:
P.O. Drawer 1088, Tarpon Springs, FL 34688; (813) 942-2000

JACKSON HOLE GOLF AND TENNIS CLUB:
5000 Spring Gulch Rd., Jackson, WY 83001; (307) 733-3111

JASPER PARK LODGE:
P.O. Box 40, Jasper, Alberta, Canada T0E 1E0; (403) 852-3301

KANANASKIS COUNTRY GOLF COURSE:
P.O. Box 1710, Kananaskis Village, Alberta, Canada T0L 2H0; (403) 591-7070

KEMPER LAKES GOLF COURSE:
Old McHenry Rd., Hawthorn Woods, IL 60047; (708) 540-3450

KIAWAH ISLAND:
P.O. Box 2941201, Kiawah Island, SC 29412; (803) 768-2529

KINGSMILL GOLF CLUB:
100 Golf Club Road, Williamsburg, VA 23185; (804) 253-3906

LA COSTA HOTEL & SPA:
Costa Del Mar Rd., Carlsbad, CA 92009; (619) 438-9111

LAS HADAS:
APDO. Postal 51, Manzanillo 28200, Colima, Mexico; (333) 30000

MAUNA KEA BEACH HOTEL:
One Mauna Kea Beach Dr., Kohala Coast, HI 96743; (808) 882-7222

MAUNA LANI RESORT:
P.O. Box 4959, Kohala Coast, HI 96743; (808) 885-6677

PASATIEMPO GOLF CLUB:
18 Clubhouse Rd., Santa Cruz, CA 95061; (408) 426-3622

PEBBLE BEACH GOLF LINKS:
P.O. Box 658, Pebble Beach, CA 93953; (408) 624-3811

PGA WEST:
56-150 PGA Blvd., La Quinta, CA 92253; (619) 564-7429

PINEHURST NO. 2:
Pinehurst Golf & Country Club, P.O. Box 4000, Pinehurst, NC 28374; (919) 295-6811

PINEHURST NO. 7:
Pinehurst Golf & Country Club, P.O. Box 4000, Pinehurst, NC 28374; (919) 295-6811

THE PIT GOLF LINKS:
P.O. Box 3006 McIntyre Station, Pinehurst, NC 28374; (919) 944-1600

SEA ISLAND GOLF CLUB:
The Cloister, Sea Island, GA 31561; (912) 638-5118

THE RESORT SEMIAHMOO:
9550 Semiahmoo Parkway, Blaine, WA 98230; (206) 371-5100

THE LINKS AT SPANISH BAY:
17 Mile Dr., Pebble Beach, CA 93953; (800) 654-9300

SPYGLASS HILL GOLF COURSE:
P.O. Box 658, Pebble Beach, CA 93953; (408) 625-8563

TANGLEWOOD PARK:
Highway 158 West, P.O. Box 1040, Clemmons, NC 27012; (919) 766-5082

TETON PINES:
Star Route Box 3669, Jackson, Wyoming 83001; (307) 733-1733

TIDEWATER GOLF CLUB & PLANTATION:
4901 Little River Neck Rd., North Myrtle Beach, SC 29582; (803) 249-3829

TOKATEE GOLF CLUB:
Blue River, OR 97413; (503) 822-3220

TORREY PINES:
11480 North Torrey Pines Rd., La Jolla, CA 92009; (619) 438-9111

TOURNAMENT PLAYERS CLUB:
110 TPC Boulevard, Ponte Vedra, FL 32082; (904) 273-3235

TOURNAMENT PLAYERS CLUB SCOTTSDALE:
17020 North Hayden Rd., Scottsdale, AZ 85255; (602) 585-3939

TROON NORTH:
10320 East Dynamite Boulevard, Scottsdale, AZ 85255; (602) 585-5300

TRYALL GOLF CLUB:
Sandy Bay P.O., Parish of Hanover, Jamaica, West Indies; (809) 952-5110

VENTANA CANYON:
7000 N. Resort Dr., Tucson, AZ 85715; (602) 577-6258

WILD DUNES:
P.O. Box 388, Isle of Palms, SC 29402; (803) 886-6000

PHOTO CREDITS

INDEX BY PAGE

INDEX BY PHOTOGRAPHER

Acknowledgements

Special thanks to all those representing the golf courses who assisted the publishers in the preparation of this book, and to the freelance photographers whose pictures help bring these courses to life, especially Jim Moriarty, Tony Roberts, Larry Petrillo, Joanne Dost, Bill Woodward, Lloyd Aaron. The publishers would also like to extend their special thanks to Robert Trent Jones, Sr. and Red Hoffman for their support with this project. The designer of this book, Mark Weinberg, wishes to thank Les Garland, James Rizzi, Gib Smith, Mark Ruchstuhl, Craig Cole, Gil Kendricks, Glenn O'Brien, Scott Cohen, Topsy Siderowf, Tim, Stu, Todd, Larry, Richie, and Susan for their encouragement and patience.